USSR

gan

Mashhad

Nishapur

KHORASAN

Herat

avir

Tabas

A   N

AFGHANISTAN

zd

Dasht-e Lut

K

Zahedan

TAN   P   STA

Ban

Str. of Hormoz

OMAN

U.A.E.

An
Ambassador's
Wife
in Iran

An Ambassador's Wife in Iran

CYNTHIA HELMS

DODD, MEAD & COMPANY

NEW YORK

119973

1 2 3 4 5 6 7 8 9 10

Library of Congress Cataloging in Publication Data

Helms, Cynthia.
   An ambassador's wife in Iran.

   Includes index.
   1.   Iran—Description and travel.   2.   Helms, Cynthia.
I.   Title.
DS259.H44   955'.05   80-25090
ISBN 0-396-07881-8

For the future pleasure of
six very special short people:
Jack, Katie, Meg, Cynthia (C2), Emily, and Rory.

Contents

List of Illustrations

Preface

When it was first suggested that I write a book about Iran, I was startled at the idea. But as I began to think about it seriously and to listen to the questions of friends and acquaintances as they became more and more aware of that country, I decided that I would try to convey some of my experiences in the hope that they would bring a greater familiarity with a part of the world which seems so often in the newspapers or on television. It is rare to find two people who agree on anything about Iran; but as an American friend said to me, "Once you've lived in Iran, you're never quite the same again."

I have written this book not as a scholar, but as a "roving stranger." Fittingly, even these words, which I had first chosen as a title for this book, come from a Persian poem.

I would like to thank Alexander Burnham, managing editor of Dodd, Mead and Company, for his faith in the book. He contributed invaluable advice and considerable final editing. I should also like to thank

Patricia Cecil Hass for her editorial assistance and for her special insights into the organization of the material.

In an effort to be as accurate as possible, each chapter has been read by at least two Iran scholars, some of whom are Iranian citizens. I am most grateful for the time they have taken to read the manuscript and for their comments and suggestions. Because of the current political tension between our two countries, and to avoid any criticism of their involvement in my opinions, I would like to express my appreciation to them without listing their names.

With the encouragement of my dear beloved husband and patient steadfast friend, Richard Helms, I have written about Iran the way I came to know it.

There are many different ways to spell Persian names and terms. The system used here is based on the way these names and terms are actually pronounced by educated Iranians in the capital, Tehran. This means that pronunciations more reflective of Arabic than Persian, e.g. Isfahan (Arabic), Esfahan (Persian), or ones that have no foundation in the Persian language, e.g. Teheran, are strictly excluded. In a few cases, however, words of Arabic origin (especially ones relating to the Islamic religion) that are better known in the West in their Arabic forms than in their Persian forms, e.g. *imam* (Arabic), *emam* (Persian), are used to facilitate reader recognition.

C.H.

Washington, D.C.
September 1980

1

A Change
of Scene

*Until you take the plunge you will never become
a swimmer.* *

On November 20, 1972, I came home to our Washington apartment, opened the door, and was surprised to find my husband already there. He was silhouetted against the window, looking out at the trees behind our living room.

"The President is appointing a new director of Central Intelligence," he said.

I sat down. It was not unexpected. Richard Nixon had just been reelected and he was making other changes among his top aides and administrators. Dick described the Camp David interview, reminding me that President Nixon was never very good at small talk. In a mumbling way the President had noted that, although he had reappointed Dick in 1968, the original appointment was by another President, a Democrat.

*The lines that follow each chapter opening are traditional Persian proverbs.

Dick told the President he well understood this, and went on to say, "I'm almost sixty, or I will be at the end of March. That might be a good time for me to leave."

Nixon said he had not realized it was CIA policy to retire personnel at that age, and in fact seemed very surprised that Dick was almost sixty. When Nixon learned that Dick had been in government service since 1942 and in Intelligence since 1943, he was nonplussed. It was obvious he knew nothing about Dick's past career.

Suddenly, as if it were a totally new idea—Dick felt that it had never crossed the President's mind before—Nixon said, "Would you like to be an ambassador?"

Dick replied that the possibility had not occurred to him; he would need some time to think about it. The President continued talking, with no real continuity to his remarks, and then came back to the same thought, pressing Dick again.

"If you were going to become an ambassador, where would you want to go?" Nixon asked.

After thinking for just a second or two, Dick said, "Iran."

Nixon appeared thoughtful and then said, "Yes, that would be all right. We have something else in mind for Joe Farland." (Ambassador Joseph Farland was there at the time.)

Then the President made a strange suggestion. "Why don't you go as ambassador to the Soviet Union?"

Dick said he was astonished. He realized Nixon was quite serious. Dick answered quietly that considering his background he would be reluctant to go there. The President nodded his head in agreement and after a little more discussion Dick agreed to think about going to Iran.

Dick had been in government for thirty years. We had already discussed his eventual retirement and had made plans to announce it the following spring. We had bought a small house in Washington to move into and were looking forward to a period of less pressure and more time for recreation.

Now Dick looked at me. Would I like to go to Iran? Iran? Why would we want to go to Iran? Born and raised in Britain, I had come to America at the age of twenty-three and had always nurtured an unrequited desire to live on the European continent. Why hadn't he chosen Europe?

"Because," Dick said, "Iran is an area where the influences of both East and West come to bear. With the West's increasing need for oil and the Shah's plans for his country's modernization, I think it would be challenging to be there at this extraordinary time."

Besides, Dick had known the Shah for many years; they had met in 1957. They had attended the same school in Switzerland, Le Rosey, but there the Shah was a contemporary of Dick's younger brother. In recent years Dick had frequently briefed His Majesty when he visited the United States.

How did I feel about the suggestion? Miserable. Selfish. Why should I want to leave my job and my children to become an unpaid working member of the diplomatic corps?

But, somewhere around the soles of my feet, the idea of living in Persia stirred a response. Was it the memory of the *Rubaiyat* of Omar Khayyam of Nishapur, and the recollection of myself as a young girl frequently turning the pages of a beautiful volume of those quatrains, coveting that volume, and finally spending more than two weeks of my navy pay to buy it for a cherished friend—the only present that I ever regretted giving? I remembered one verse in particular:

Awake! for morning in the Bowl of Night
Has flung the Stone that put the Stars to Flight;
And Lo! the Hunter of the East has caught
The Sultan's Turret in a Noose of Light.

Perhaps now I would be able to go to Nishapur and find that very Sultan's turret.

Other thoughts came to mind from books I had read: *Persia and the Persians* by the first American minister to serve in Persia, who described glowingly summer camping in the Lar Valley; *Arabesque and Honeycomb,* where Sacheverell Sitwell wrote of the "indescribable excitement" he felt at his first glimpse of the blue and gold mosques of Mashhad. He had waited unsuccessfully for several days, hoping to be allowed to go into the famous shrine. Could I possibly, twenty years later, be allowed to enter?

Dick and I talked for hours and decided finally to go. Dick called the White House in due course to say he would accept the appointment as ambassador to Iran. Bill Rogers, the Secretary of State, telephoned to confirm his acceptance and said he would cable the Shah to request his agreement. It came within twenty-four hours. We were committed.

There was a space of several weeks before the public announcement that Dick was to leave the Central Intelligence Agency. Then his ambassadorial appointment would have to be confirmed by the Senate. Until this happened we could not proceed with any logistical moving plans, which gave me time to quietly wind up my job.

I had worked at the Smithsonian in one capacity or another for seven years, first at the National Portrait Gallery and the Anacostia Neighborhood Museum, and then for four years at the Museum of History and Technology under the director of the Office of Public Affairs. I was in charge of programs for Radio Smithsonian, which included supervising the research and doing the broadcasts myself. The program was heard locally in Washington, on 150 stations across the country, and on the Armed Forces Radio overseas. Its thrust were lectures by interesting guests, curators, and researchers, and talks on the thousand and one subjects covered by the Smithsonian professional staff.

It was a fascinating job, and I hated to leave it. I had interviewed hundreds of interesting people, from Edward Teller, the nuclear physicist, to Saul Bellow. Most of my radio listeners seemed to enjoy the program, although one day a man from Wisconsin wrote to say that he didn't like my voice, and what was more, he had twenty-three friends who didn't like it either. Perhaps he didn't like my pronunciation. Even though I had lived in America for many years I still had lapses over the pronunciation of some words. I was despondent for the whole day and then bought myself a dictionary of English/American pronunciation. After that I wrote him a card to say he was lucky to have twenty-three friends, filed the letter under "vituperations" (the only such letter, I'm glad to say), and consoled myself that he probably had a relative who wanted my job.

But now I had many new things to think about. Dick and I were going to lead a very different life. What should we take with us? What would our days be like? I needed hats to wear when the Empress received me for an audience, clothes suitable for a Moslem country, for desert travel, and for the rural areas. But Iran is also mountainous and there is snow in the winter. Bill Blass, the designer, agreed to advise me. Dick came with me to Bill's New York showrooms and was very helpful, too, until actress Faye Dunaway appeared on the other side of the clothes racks and diverted his attention.

Dick smugly announced he wouldn't need new formal attire when he presented his credentials at the Court in Tehran. He could still wear the carefully preserved striped pants made for him for a wedding in London in 1935!

There were other questions more important than clothes, and I needed answers. For these I went to our friends in the U.S. diplomatic corps.

David Bruce had been ambassador to France, Great Britain, and Germany and was soon to go to China to head the mission there. He made two invaluable suggestions. First, reduce the guest list for the Fourth of July, celebrated by all U.S. embassies, to a minimum. Don't listen to any arguments from the embassy staff about this. The guest list can get far too big and this will leave you without adequate funds for entertaining the rest of the year.

Second, be careful who you invite to stay with you. In an embassy all expenses incurred at the residence by friends who come as house guests are the ambassador's responsibility. So, too, are official guests unless they are of very high rank, such as the Secretary of State and his party. A special allowance is made to cover the expenses of these guests. So, invite old friends and official guests to stay with you and give the rest only dinner.

As director of Central Intelligence, Dick had not had an official house, so I had not been used to running a government residence. While I had certainly run a large family household and had been used to the nuances of protocol when we entertained, I knew that running an embassy would be very different.

In every country the official residence differs. We were shown photographs of our "home" in Tehran. It was large, but fortunately built as an embassy residence, not a converted house. It contained large reception rooms on the first floor and four big bedrooms upstairs. On the second floor a separate apartment provided some privacy for the ambassador and his family. But single beds for four years? Never! We ordered no new furniture, except we courageously asked for a new king-sized bed. Furniture, carpets, and draperies are supplied and maintained by the Foreign Buildings Office of the State Department.

Nothing is supplied in the way of graphic arts for those large bare walls in the reception rooms, so I went to see Mr. and Mrs. Stanley Woodward. He was previously ambassador to Canada. Realizing the wonderful opportunity embassies have to exhibit American art in foreign countries, he and his wife had formed a foundation. I went to their house in Georgetown and selected paintings and prints. They lent us works by such diverse artists as Jasper Johns, Robert Rauschenberg, Bill Walton, Willem de Kooning, Larry Rivers, Josef Albers, Milton Avery, and many other popular and well-known American artists. This not only gave us personal pleasure, but a chance to entertain many Iranian artists, as there were no other such collections in Iran.

Next I went to see Joshua Taylor, director of the National Collection of Fine Arts (part of the Smithsonian). I asked him to lend us a few of George Catlin's paintings of Indians and the West. He said he would be delighted to, but he thought I would have trouble extracting them from the curators. The paintings had been lent in prior years to embassies and unfortunately had not been well taken care of, and the curators were loath to lend them again. He was right. But using all my powers of persuasion, I was allowed to borrow six paintings—certainly not the finest, but at least we had some to exhibit. I chose scenes of the American West, because this is an area of our country that fascinates many foreigners, and most of them are unfamiliar with it.

Finally, I went to the Freer Gallery, again part of the Smithsonian, which houses one of the world's most distinguished collections of Oriental art. There Dr. Esin Atil, curator of the Islamic collection, taught me how to look at the intricate detail of Oriental art. She explained how the marginal decorations on the manuscript in the *moraqqa,* or the albums, could be more interesting than the painting in the center; how to look at the intricacy of detail in some miniatures, only comprehended after hours of study; how the pottery sometimes represents an animal that is not discernible at first glance; how to examine glazes on the Islamic pieces.

She introduced me to Kufic writing and its sensual artistic form, and said that she was now sure it had been used for more than the religious writings previously presumed. By the time Dr. Atil had finished with me I was so excited at the possibilities of studying in Persia that it softened the withdrawal pains caused by leaving home.

Now there was only one last worry—leaving my four children behind. Two were married, but my youngest daughter, Lindsay, was only twenty and my son "Bones," twenty-two, was not "settled" in any definable way. I told him I had hung my portrait in our beach house and from that vantage point I expected to keep an eye on his activities. He admitted to me later that that portrait had more of an impact than an untold number of lectures.

Our pace quickened. Dick was briefed on his new duties. Books, family photographs, treasures we couldn't bear to live without, calling cards, and boxes of blank invitations that filled me with trepidation were shipped to Tehran. We took one last vacation with our children and on our way through Texas we stopped to say good-bye to former President and Mrs. Johnson. He said that if we would let them know when we were settled, they would come out to Tehran for a visit. That was on December 20, 1972. On January 22 he died.

Our farewell parties were over; we had said good-bye to friends. Our own furniture went into storage and we were ready to leave. In a last-minute call an officer of the State Department inquired if I had been informed that ambassadors had to supply all the salt and pepper shakers for their embassies. I had not. I raced out to buy enough for a dining room table that seated thirty-six.

After Senate confirmation of the appointment, there is a swearing-in ceremony for a newly appointed ambassador held on the eighth floor of the State Department. "Bones" offered to drive me in his jeep to the ceremony, presided over by Bill Rogers.

Descending from the jeep's metal steps, squeezed in between long black limousines, clutching the salt and pepper shakers in the hope that I could find somebody to dispatch them in the diplomatic pouch to Tehran, I concluded that my execution of the duties of an ambassador's wife needed improvement.

The last telephone call we received before our departure was the notice from the director general of the Foreign Service. He informed Dick that if he were kidnapped by terrorists, he should not expect to be ransomed.

2

The Embassy:
A New Home

A bird once liberated from its cage finds a garden everywhere.

Flying over western Iran en route to the capital city of Tehran, the physical dimensions of the country are immediate. Iran is like a bowl, surrounded by mountain chains, with Tehran lying at the southern edge of the Alborz range. Snow-covered in winter, excellent for skiing, the Alborz are dominated by Mount Damavand, forty miles northeast of the city. Volcanic Damavand is an almost perfect cone shape, rising from low foothills to 18,955 feet. It is higher than Mount Ararat in Turkey, and after the Himalayas, the highest peak in Asia and in Europe.

To the south beyond Tehran, where packs of wild dogs hunt, the terrain drifts away to the flat wastes and low white domes of the Dasht-e Kavir, the vast salt desert. On our arrival, huge building cranes dotted the expanse of dun-colored bare terrain to the north. The cranes were stretching to touch Shemiran, a town in the foothills of the mountains. Once Shemiran was the location of summer residences and large gardens; now it was rapidly becoming part of large, dusty, overcrowded Tehran.

As our plane circled to land at Tehran's Mehrabad Airport, the Sasanian-inspired arch of the Shahyad monument, designed by a young Iranian and built to celebrate the twenty-five-hundredth anniversary of the country, rose to greet us. It was our first evidence of the very old and the very new that combine in today's Persia.

In the mid-seventies air travel increased enormously, and because of the great distance and the time changes from Europe or India and the East, many planes landed in the early morning or late at night. Whatever the hour, there was always a seething mass of people at the airport, wearing anything from blue jeans to the veil.

Our plane landed late in the evening. We were welcomed at the ramp by members of the embassy staff and representatives of the Iranian Foreign Office, and a frightening sea of unknown faces. I wondered if they were all friendly.

During our stopover in Geneva, we had been awakened in the middle of the night by a call from the U.S. embassy in Switzerland. An official told Dick they had a warning that the Black September were after him. The Black September is one of the clandestine terrorist arms of the Palestine Liberation Organization; its name derives from the September in 1970 when King Hussein of Jordan turned his bedouin troops against the Palestine Liberation Army in Amman. The Munich massacre at the Olympic games in 1972 was also attributed to the Black September group, and just two weeks earlier, on March 2, they had killed the American ambassador and the deputy chief of mission in Khartoum, Sudan.

In Geneva I had heard Dick say, "Let them come, I'm going back to sleep," and after an explanation to me he did. I stayed awake. Now Dick seemed perfectly calm as Haikaz, the ambassador's chauffeur, led us to our car. It was an armor-plated Chevrolet rather than the traditional black limousine, and as a security precaution we were not flying the American flag on the right front fender. Because of the rising guerrilla movement and the increase in terrorism, we were protected by a bevy of guards supplied on orders of the Shah. We were all aware that an attempt had been made on the life of one of Dick's predecessors, Ambassador Douglas MacArthur, nephew of the famous World War II general. The captain of the guards rode in the seat beside Haikaz. Another car containing four guards traveled behind the Chevrolet. Haikaz maneuvered along the road through an interesting composite of cars, goats, sheep, and the occasional camel train bearing fertilizer, and into the traffic of Tehran.

The embassy residence was surrounded by a compound of twenty-five acres. The offices of the embassy bordered on Takht-e Jamshid Avenue. The driveway brought us past the rose garden to the large Persian blue front doors banked by tubs of oleander shrubs.

Bought in 1928 for sixty thousand dollars, water rights included, at 1973's land prices the residence had become one of the best investments made by the United States government for an embassy abroad. Sold to pay off a gambling debt, it was at one time the summer residence of a family who used the compound to escape the heat and dust of the old city.

When we arrived it was like an oasis in the middle of downtown Tehran. Fountains adorned the garden and freshly watered grass grew in abundance under the tall pine and sycamore trees. I looked around and took a deep breath. Here was a different house, a different culture, a different way of life, and all of it would be lived with associates I had never met. I was a little overwhelmed.

Dick squeezed my hand. "You'll be fine," he said. "You'll have it all under control in no time."

"I hope so," I said, smiling at him.

For an ambassador's wife, the first few weeks in an embassy can be overwhelming. Like a child's drawing of the sun and its rays, I had to go in all directions at once.

As ambassador, Dick had to present his credentials to the chief of state. (If he had left them in his baggage, they might not have come for weeks, which would have been traumatic and even considered a bad omen.) Otherwise we had only our two suitcases, carefully packed because in them were the clothes we needed for every occasion until our freight arrived.

Our living quarters were upstairs—four large bedrooms for guests and our own private apartment: a sitting room, a bedroom, and a bathroom with a large black marble bath installed by one of our predecessors. We were charged a monthly rent for this apartment, but it was a haven of privacy.

We had shipped our books and our prints with my porcelain, all the touches that would make us feel at home, and until they came our rooms

The embassy residence in Tehran where Dick and I lived for nearly four years.

seemed bare and lonely. I moved some of the furniture and put flowers everywhere. I also set up several desks—one for household business and accounts, another for personal mail, a third for language study, and a fourth for Dick. I ended up using his most of the time as it was the only one with any empty space. Next I exchanged some of the furniture in the reception rooms for pieces I found sitting unused in the embassy warehouse. (One ambassador's wife wants gold candles everywhere; another finds them anathema.)

Our small family dining room had a glorious view of the mountains, but it needed table linen, which was not supplied by the government. The large state dining room had one long table that could be broken up into smaller ones. It seated thirty-six, but I could find only one set of old place mats. There were piles of table cloths in the cupboard, but they didn't fit any of the tables.

I asked a number of embassy aides if we could order new table linens. The rather shocking reply was that unless Congress appropriated funds for that particular purpose, we could not! But our need was immediate, since we were expecting a large group of visitors. So I set off with my guard for the bazaar, returning laden with hand-blocked material called *qalamkar,* as well as a taste for using local materials and colors. Sometimes it was the only way to operate. When I wanted to cover some old camel-colored wrought-iron furniture, I went again to the administration officer asking for funds. He said authority would be needed from the Foreign Buildings Office in Washington, and if funds had not been appropriated for that particular purpose, we couldn't buy any material for these either.

It was dawning on me that I would need ingenuity in this job. This time it was back to the embassy warehouse to scout around for a suitable bolt of material. We painted the wrought iron celadon green, put the new furniture on the patio with an awning over it, and low and behold—a Persian garden we could use during the summer at no expense to the taxpayer!

The head butler, Farooq, a handsome Pakistani trained in the tradition of quiet, excellent service, ran the staff well and efficiently. I met with him and with the chef every morning to discuss menus and plans for the following day. Farooq became a fable among our house guests, but in the beginning I could not understand him. He kept looking among our belongings and saying: "The picture for the piano?"

I produced pictures of Dick, pictures of the children, and various

The embassy's resident staff. Farooq, the head butler, is second from left; Luigi, the chef, is third from left.

other friends, and placed them on the piano. But something was wrong, and Farooq was not mollified. It came to me in the middle of the night. We were not really acceptable to the staff until we presented our credentials to them: a signed picture of our President to sit on the piano. The very first thing the next morning I wrote to the White House. The picture came by return mail, and Farooq and I had no further difficulty communicating.

Luigi, the Italian chef, had been there for over twenty years. He was a superb cook of Persian, European, and American dishes. In the East, communications and travel are difficult, and sometimes I had to change our plans. Unlike many chefs, Luigi was never annoyed; he could produce an exquisite meal for many guests on a half day's notice if necessary. His only request was that meals be served on time when we entertained. Any creator of superb soufflés, and he was one, can understand this plea, but in the East it was like asking for the moon. Even so, Luigi did everything with ease and with the best of tempers, and except for continually finding ingenious reasons why he should receive more money, any frustrations he had were invisible to us.

The domestic staff was already at the residence and agreed to stay on while we were there. There were six men and one woman, and at first, when I looked for some of them in the afternoons, I couldn't understand where they disappeared to. Eventually I realized the woman was always among the missing, and I decided it would be better to have an all-male staff.

Most of the gardeners appeared to be very old. Sometimes facing Mecca to say their prayers, sometimes asleep under the benches in the greenhouses, they always watered when it was raining. To practice my Persian I would stop and talk with them about anything my limited vocabulary would allow, but soon word came back to me that they were anxiously running to the personnel office. I was asking so many questions they were afraid they had done something wrong, and when I tried to take care of a few plants myself, the gardeners felt they were losing face and nearly quit.

The head gardener asked for an appointment and nervously asked me about flowers. One former resident had wanted only short-stemmed flowers and another only long-stemmed ones. I had had visions of having to buy flowers, so I asked him just to grow as many flowers as he could for arrangements in those large rooms. Then I suggested my plan for making the potted plants attractive by painting the pots in different colors—vivid Persian blues and greens and yellows. I don't know why this plan was not appealing, but some of the pots disappeared and others were done in the wrong colors. In the end, it was silently agreed that the gardeners would look after the garden and I would look after the ambassador.

The sixteen marines assigned to guard the embassy were all very young. Commanded by a sergeant, they carried out what was a usually boring task—since then, tragically proved otherwise—with good nature, large appetites, and a diligent attitude toward planning and raising funds for their annual Marine Ball. Apart from the twenty-four-hour guard duty at the embassy, one was always assigned to all-night duty at the residence.

The guards who came with us in the cars were from the Iranian National Police, a physically fit and highly trained group. If I wanted to leave the compound either in the car or on foot, I had to request one of these men to go with me. While in the compound itself, Iranian armed guards were posted at intervals all around us. When we first arrived they were a motley crew whose appearance was not enhanced by their ill-fitting uniforms, and I thought that crossing the compound at night might be the most dangerous thing we could do. We began a campaign of extra training, less tea drinking on duty, and a more realistic tape measure, and they spruced up enormously.

Until an ambassador has presented his credentials to the head of state in the country to which he is accredited, he is not officially in residence, and the ambassador waits until he receives permission to present his credentials. When we arrived, the Shah was on holiday in the Persian Gulf on the island of Kish, but soon he returned and the grand master of ceremonies at the court called the ambassador's office to schedule the ceremony for the presentation of credentials.

At nine A.M. on the appointed day a blue Rolls Royce arrived. Dick, dressed in white tie and tails and accompanied by the chief of protocol of the Iranian Foreign Ministry, was driven to Niavaran Palace for his audience with the Shah. After the ceremony they returned to the residence for a traditional glass of champagne with all the officers in the embassy. Dick was now officially in residence as the ambassador and chief of mission of the United States in Iran.

In accordance with the requirements of protocol, Dick next had to call on Empress Farah, the Shahbanu (king's lady). This time I was invited —we were to arrive fifteen minutes ahead of schedule and I was asked to wear a hat. (Hats had to be worn for all official occasions.) A cham-

Shortly after arriving in Tehran, Dick presented his credentials to the Shah at Niavaran Palace.

berlain attired in morning coat and striped trousers met us at the door of the palace. He ushered us into a small side room to wait, reappeared at the appointed hour, and escorted us to the large salon. Exquisite Persian rugs covered the floor, but the furniture was French. Fabulous ancient artifacts were displayed in cabinets or shelves around the room. A portrait of the Shah by the American artist, William Draper, caught my eye.

Before we had time to examine the Lorestan bronzes, the doors opened and the Shahbanu entered. She was extremely attractive, slim, and poised, and she looked relaxed. Her hair was lightened and the heavy dark brows of previous years were gone. After plastic surgery, her features were finer than they appeared in the pictures taken at the time of her marriage, when she was only twenty-one.

No longer shy, she was used to receiving, and laughed and talked about her children and told anecdotes of her life as Queen. While she was talking about the difficulties of getting things done out in the country, she rang the bell for tea. When it did not arrive, she said good naturedly, "You see, even in the palace!"

I wondered how we would know when to leave, but it was not a problem. At a natural conclusion to our conversation, she rose. She said good-bye graciously and left the room first, asking an aide who was waiting outside the door to escort us to the palace gates.

The dean of the diplomatic corps is always the ambassador who has been accredited to a foreign government for the longest consecutive period. In Tehran this was the Russian ambassador, Mr. Vladimir Erofeev. We met him at our first official function, a reception at the Ministry of Foreign Affairs. When it was known my husband was coming to Iran, an article in *Time* magazine reported that the Russian had asked the Iranian prime minister how he felt about America's sending their number-one spy as ambassador. The Prime Minister, Amir Abbas Hoveyda, answered that at least America was sending its number-one spy whereas the Russians had only sent their number-ten.

Dick approached the dean at the reception to pay his respects.

"Excellency," said number one to number ten, "I understand there has been talk about us."

The Russian answered, "Yes, there has been talk about us, but I'll tell you this. You will never become number one here because I intend to stay dean as long as you are here."

Erofeev was recalled to Moscow in 1977 shortly after our departure from Iran.

In Iran the accepted system of protocol was for each new ambassador to call on each resident ambassador. This meant we had to make about seventy calls. A formidable task. It would take us months. So we decided to try to make two or three calls after office hours every day. The dean and Mrs. Erofeev had to be first. Dressed in an appropriately ambassadorial fashion, with our calling cards in hand, we set off, followed by our guards. We arrived at the large Russian compound, only a few minutes away, where a towering, silent Russian greeted us. He ushered us into a small side room where the Erofeevs were waiting for us.

Mrs. Erofeev, an attractive, lively woman from Georgia in southern Russia, asked my advice on American books that she might translate into Russian. I was about to recommend some when I remembered that the Soviet Union's copyright laws were not yet enforced. I quickly told her I would try to think of some titles, and I would phone her. I never did.

At four o'clock in the afternoon, we were served vodka. Alcohol is strictly medicinal for me, but prepared for anything in the service of my country, I drank it down. That was my first mistake. My second was to drink it quickly in what I was led to believe was the true Russian tradition. Lo and behold, another one arrived. That was my first lesson in diplomacy. We then had tea, and when the conversation lagged the ambassador suggested he show us around the compound. Perhaps I looked in need of fresh air.

The Russian compound was the site of the 1943 Tehran Conference attended by Franklin Roosevelt, Winston Churchill, and Joseph Stalin. Although the American embassy was close by, Roosevelt stayed at the Russian compound. Ambassador Charles Bohlen, who acted as interpreter at this meeting, says in his book, *Witness to History,* that this strange lodging decision was made because of possible security problems.

After tea, we walked from the residence to the building where the "Big Three" had held their meetings, a structure of large, cavernous reception halls. A burly guard unlocked the enormous doors. It was cold inside. There were high ceilings, a few carpets, and nondescript furniture placed around the walls. The ambassador explained that it was not known what had happened to the actual conference table or the chairs. They appeared to have been lost, he said with a smile.

As he talked, he took us to a side room. Signaling for the door to be opened, he said, "And here we have another conference room."

We looked in, politely interested. There was a Russian sitting huddled in a far corner. He was deep in conversation with a man apparently of different nationality. Ambassador Erofeev was obviously nervous. "Excuse me," he said to them in English and rushed us out of the building.

Solemnly, we thanked him for tea and fell into our car, chuckling long before we were outside those padlocked gates.

Driving back to the American embassy, I fell to wondering how I was going to manage the hospitable side of diplomatic life. I liked much of it—the coherent conversation for thirty minutes, the approved duration of a call, the learning about an ambassadorial couple and becoming immediately acquainted. I also liked focusing on the geographic location of some countries I couldn't remember. Even after years of geography at school, developments and independence had changed borders and names. Ceylon had become Sri Lanka and the Trucial States the United Arab Emirates (composed of sheikhdoms with romantic names of their own, Abu Dhabi and Dubai); and there were many others.

One "difficulty" was the hospitality offered by Eastern countries; it can be overwhelming. This has to be a tradition derived from welcoming visitors in the inhospitable desert. It presented a problem for me because Dick, maddeningly disciplined about what he eats, was declining all the cakes and cookies pressed upon us—and I seemed to be making up for him.

The final straw came the day we called on the ambassador from the United Arab Emirates and his wife, both in their twenties. It was our second call that day. Their cook had worked for an American couple in one of the other Persian Gulf countries, and he must have spent the whole week preparing for us. The kitchen door opened and the smiling, proud chef wheeled in a large trolley, laden with cakes and cookies; he must have cooked one of everything listed in the cakes and cookies section of *Joy of Cooking*.

When we finally poured ourselves into the car, I was certain I couldn't make it home. I felt like a human fountain—if you poked me, some of the tea, juice, coffee, cakes, and cookies would come out of my ears. Through enveloping nausea I announced firmly to the American ambassador that we were going to change the system: When the newly appointed couples began to call on us, we were going to invite them to a slimming, dietetic lunch.

3

Tehran: A City of Conflict

One cannot fly with other people's wings.

Tehran is a large, sprawling city with a population approaching five million. To the hasty eye, it is a modern city with streets clogged by traffic jams. Yet, it is also primitive, lacking even a central sewage system. Lying just north of the old silk route from the Far East, Tehran was once a winter shelter, pasture, and trading post frequented by nomads. In 1788 it was made the Persian capital by the eunuch Aqa Mohammad, the cruel first Shah of the Qajars, the ruling dynasty immediately preceding the Pahlavis. It is not a charming city, but it was redeemed for me by the complex impressions that rushed at my mind and senses as I explored the streets.

In the eighteenth century, Aqa Mohammad repaired the old city walls and fortifications and built six magnificent arched gates of colorful glazed bricks. He placed these gates in a geometrical design leading to all the main routes out of the city, so the old city was virtually a royal stronghold. The American minister, S. S. W. Benjamin, who opened our first legation in Tehran in 1883, spoke of a burgeoning walled city of two hundred thousand people. Today wide avenues, often lined with plane trees, expand Tehran north and south from the old citadel. One of these, Ferdowsi Avenue, is full of shops, bustling pedestrians, and the ever-present traffic struggling to negotiate Ferdowsi Square.

Ferdowsi was a poet. His statue stands in the center of the square, the figure of a man calmly holding a book while the turmoil of modern Tehran swirls around him. There was turmoil as well in the late tenth century when a tribe called the Seljuks swept into power, and Ferdowsi wrote the national epic *Shahnameh.* I found it refreshing to think that a people would name its streets after poets, and more refreshing still to realize that every Iranian can quote poetry. Taxi drivers, statesmen, shepherds—all seem to have a truly national feeling about it.

I also found, when I began to go out into the city, that the accepted way to manage the traffic congestion was to assume you were on the Indianapolis Speedway. Any free space you saw ahead, no matter if it was three lanes over, was yours for the occupying. Cars weave back and forth or make sudden U-turns in front of you without warning, changing lanes constantly. Wild motorcyclists do daily what stunt men consider daring and, in addition, regard sidewalks as their thoroughfares. Minor car accidents, of which there are many, are negotiated on the spot, although settlement is not necessarily for the person with the right of way.

I began my explorations in the old city at the Golestan, the fortified palace begun by Aqa Mohammad and finished by his successor, Fath Ali Shah, who is said to have fathered 240 children and was considered a capable ruler in spite of his vanity and avarice. The Golestan was restored in 1967 when the late Shah finally held his coronation. High walls surround an open pavillion, where the Shahs of past dynasties received in oriental splendor. Benjamin wrote of seeing an enormous folio of the *Arabian Nights* there when he was received by Naser od-Din Shah. The *andarun,* where the wives lived, and the grand audience chamber were still used for state visits and receptions when Dick and I were in Iran. Filled with incredibly ornate gifts sent to the Shahs through the years, the glazed tile floors were covered with priceless Persian carpets, and mosaics of mirror glass decorated the main rooms and entrance halls. (Mosaics are a formal decoration used now in mosques and palaces. In the Iranian embassy in Washington there is even a mirror room created with tiny mirror mosaics, an art form that evolved from the days when mirrors ordered from Venice arrived broken so often that artisans fashioned the shattered pieces into decorations called *a'ineh kari.*)

At the Golestan, more than any other place in Iran, I sensed the ancient life of the oriental Court. I strolled, enchanted, beside the marble pools, wondering what it must have been like when Shahs long since gone and their retinues received in the gardens on rich carpets piled high with baskets of fruit, sweetmeats, nuts, and *sharbat,* a cooling drink. The tall trees and the gardens were still there; so sometimes were dignitaries and courtiers, although they could seldom match the colorful personages of the past. The library remained, however, with a wealth of beautifully illuminated manuscripts and *moraqqas,* handwritten by the famous old calligraphers.

Ferdowsi's work was there, handed down along with that of other Persian poets of centuries past. Even though the late Shah's father was a great admirer of Kemal Atatürk, he did not change the script of the Iranian language as Atatürk had done in Turkey. This is one of the reasons Persian literature has been so well preserved, and the old manuscripts can still be read by all literate students. But sadly, many manuscripts have been lost. In the seventeenth century the library was completely neglected and many of the titles were stolen and went to other countries. Some years ago parts of this valuable collection—including a book from the thirteenth century—were found neglected, mildewed, and randomly stacked in an unused room of the Golestan. Some, fortunately, were still in good enough condition for cataloging and preservation.

There is another fabled collection in Tehran, and it had quite a different effect on me. These were the crown jewels. Displayed in a vaultlike room under the Bank Markazi, mounds of uncut stones—diamonds, emeralds, rubies—lay in glass cases protected by devices that set off loud clanging alarms if anyone touched them.

I looked at spinels and stones set in tiaras; *qaliyans* (smoking pipes) and jewel-encrusted swords; and a globe inlaid with over fifty-one thousand precious stones. There were ropes of pearls and men's robes fit for any dandy, but very few sapphires. I discovered an exquisite emerald box, surely the most beautiful piece in the whole extravagant collection, valued some years ago at five million dollars.

The crown jewels represented the wealth and power of the kingdom and in past epochs they were carried with the king. One nineteenth-century Shah particularly enjoyed their splendor and preferred to amass the jewels rather than use them to pay his armies. Many of these jewels were brought from India as the spoils of war to emblazon the coronation robe and crown of the Shahs. Before the new oil wealth they served as backing for seventy-five percent of all Iranian currency. In 1969 the Shah conferred legal title to them on the government of Iran. After that the royal family could still borrow pieces, but they had to be withdrawn in the presence of two senators, two representatives from the Majlis (Parliament), Iran's solicitor general, and the Central Bank's governor. Before the Shah's overthrow, there were three thrones in Tehran. The marble throne and the so-called peacock throne, covered with gold and precious stones, are now in Golestan Palace, while the Nader throne—named after Nader Shah, an eighteenth-century ruler—is with the crown jewel collection. Of the three, the peacock throne is the most famous, but how it got its name is uncertain, although some attribute it to a concubine of Fath Ali Shah. Her name was Tavus, which means peacock in Persian.

Such opulence, all in one place, overwhelmed me. I felt surfeited and I no longer had any desire to own even a single jewel. What fascinated me more, perhaps because it was such a contrast, was the bazaar, an area of Tehran of bustling, vibrant humanity. There are six miles of covered streets and alleys wending through a labyrinth of shops. I was drawn to it by everything I had ever read or heard.

I went with a friend who knew it well, past the gold shops, through the courtyards where goods are unloaded, and past the noisy banging of the copper and metal area. We edged by loaded donkeys and human beasts of burden, smelling the spices, and aware of the constant hum of prayers. We came, quite suddenly, upon a large house where my friend had grown up. It was now a museum that housed her father's extensive collection of rare books and coins.

The bazaar is not just a collection of small shops owned by lower-class merchants. It embraces artisans, craftsmen, small businessmen, and wealthy merchants; they have interests in agriculture, construction, and the nation's burgeoning industries. Until a generation ago, the bazaar was the nerve center of Iranian society. As the country's economy has changed, the importance of the bazaar in Tehran and other cities has not diminished. It has only shifted.

The bazaar's money-lending business is still worth billions of rials a year. The merchants finance a nationwide network of Islamic schools, subsidize the publication of books, and pay much of the budgets of the

A typical copper shop in an Iranian bazaar. (IDES VAN DER GRACHT)

theological colleges in Tehran, Qom, Mashhad, Shiraz, Rey, and many other localities. Eighty percent of the financial resources put at the disposal of the Shi'ite clergy every year comes from the bazaars. The merchants contribute to orphanages, have special funds for widows and the needy, and advance capital for farmers in the rural areas.

The bazaar has its own informal system of leadership that has developed over the centuries. There are never any elections, but leaders emerge through their piety, age, helpfulness, and wisdom. These leaders insure that the bazaar is still an efficient organization. They organize religious gatherings and constitute the best network of information—the rumors in the bazaar are worth listening to—because nowadays every bazaar's leaders out in the countryside are only a telephone call away from each other.

Perhaps because of the vast wealth accumulated and because until a few years ago they were the only large social group able to afford higher education for their children, an unusually high proportion of the new "intellectual elite" was related to the bazaari (merchants of the bazaar). Many of these families intermarry, and this gives them a further strength, social cohesion, and political solidarity.

I knew I would be returning often to the bazaar, taking friends and official visitors, or browsing for myself. I was also drawn to Ferdowsi Avenue, nearer the embassy, where the carpet shops were located. By now I had had my fill of the traffic jams—vast, honking messes—and rather than sit in the back of my car with my adrenalin rising while I inhaled fumes, I often slipped out of the compound and walked.

The security officer had strong objections. He said I would get lost, that I didn't understand Eastern ways. But I settled the direction problem by noting that the mountains to the north of Tehran, changing color throughout the day (and sometimes disappearing behind the midday haze of dust and smoke), would remain as faithful direction finders.

The Eastern customs were another matter. Before I looked at the shops or the people, I had to first learn to walk along a public thoroughfare in a male-dominated society. I was dressed in modest Western clothes, but that wasn't the problem. I needed to think differently. I had to walk around the men or step off the curb if they were walking two or three abreast. I found myself being bumped and even gently pushed. Nobody was prepared to pause as I crossed the streets, not the Mercedes cars bumper to bumper with the Iranian Paykans cars, nor the truck full of workers warming their hands on a fire they had lit (was it really burning right over the fuel tank?), nor the motorcyclists weaving in and out past a small flock of sheep and goats. Tehran's policemen, who changed duty not with a nod but with a kiss, offered no assistance.

The streets were clean, but the smells were, well, pungent. A man might squat to relieve himself, and clothes were sometimes worn twenty-four hours a day. But I loved the sights and sounds—the vendors selling hot cooked beets, the wagons of steaming chestnuts, the street conversations in Persian and, occasionally, Armenian. As I walked along the streets, I was intoxicated by the sights and babble of Tehran.

In the business district, I observed dark-haired, dark-eyed women, dressed in Western clothes with a great sense of style, hurrying to shops or offices. They were elegant and often slim; the days when fat was considered beautiful in Iran were gone. Elsewhere in the city many of the women were wearing the traditional chador, the veil that covers all but the face and the hands. Indeed, the chador was not a garment forced on women by the Ayatollah Khomeini after the Shah was deposed. First worn in the days before Mohammad to protect the honor of women, it had become an article of clothing used for many purposes. It could cover blue jeans and miniskirts or keep street dust from dark Eastern eyes; it could, on occasion, be worn with a flirtatious gesture, or it could be a symbol of religious belief. It could hide less than attractive features or be used by a lovelorn lady on her way to an assignation. It has even been known to hide a man. But most women wearing the chador were hurrying along to do their marketing, and they did not tarry to glance aimlessly in the shops.

I learned to negotiate the *jubes,* which are small open waterways that still carry much of the washing and drinking water to the poorer areas of town. The water comes from the mountains by way of streams and what are called *qanats*—the ancient underground irrigation system still in use throughout much of Iran. The *jubes* are narrow but deep and dangerous for cars and pedestrians. In a country where water is precious and none is wasted, all sorts of things might get washed in the *jubes.* The strawberries sold by street vendors look so inviting until you see them being "freshened up" in the *jubes,* along with cars and not-so-clean babies. By the time the water flows from the north side of town to the south side, it is of questionable quality.

On Ferdowsi Avenue I enjoyed walking past the Jewish merchants having friendly arguments over the condition or age of prized carpets. Most of them spoke some English and welcomed a visitor with a glass of tea. They would tell me that a Persian carpet was to be looked at, felt, and understood. Buying one was not a commercial enterprise; it was the entering into of a tender, loving relationship, and it would be spoiled if one bought when lust was heavy and knowledge light.

The climate in Iran had something to do with the development of the famous Persian carpets. In the damp of Europe furniture was invented to sit on, but in the arid regions of the Iranian plateau people sit on the ground. Furniture, like knives and forks, are recent additions to a household in Iran. There are many rooms without furniture, but there are carpets stretching from wall to wall.

What makes some Persian carpets desirable and more valuable than others? Partly, of course, it is the design. Where rugmakers get their inspiration remains a mystery. Maybe from their imagination, oral tradition, and environment. The floral designs from Tabriz or Sanandaj are quite different from the floral designs from Mashhad. The geometric designs produced by the tribes differ from each other. The prayer rugs have at one end of their design an arch which resembles the *mehrab,* or prayer niche, in a mosque. In Na'in, a lovely village near Esfahan, rugs of soft blues and grays are made in both wool and silk. These are pleasingly fresh to many Western eyes.

The wool comes from the fat tailed sheep, which may be the best in the world for making rugs. The thousands of knots are tied with lightning speed, sometimes by small children. Copies of Persian rugs made in other countries seldom match the quality or pattern and coloring of the authentic Persian rugs. From the design it is possible to tell where a carpet is made and to know the traditional quality from that area.

You win the respect of the merchants when you can tell where a rug came from. It takes time but it is infinitely rewarding, because only then do they treat you as a friend and not as a tourist. To become knowledgeable, you must go from shop to shop, examining every knot. I discovered that the thinner, tightly knotted rugs are often much more valuable than the thick pile ones with less knots. Tribal pieces, flat woven *gelims* (kilims), pile carpets, and animal trappings all have their own devoted group of collectors. Sometimes the older pieces colored with vegetable dye are preferable. Whatever the kind of rug, it is a form of investment to a Persian, and nothing is bought with more care.

The shops closed down at one-thirty in the afternoon. Lunch, the main meal of the day, was often eaten with hot fresh bread from the many small bakeries. There were different kinds of unleavened flat

Pottery is a local industry at this village near Na'in.

bread and leavened *barbari*, the batter named for a group of Berbers that settled in Tehran. *Sangak* is another kind of bread. It is cooked by stretching the flat dough on stones *(sang)*.

One day at lunch I persuaded Marie Foroughi, an Iranian friend, to take me to the baths. Iranians love the baths, known as the *hammam*. We were shown into a tiled room, very hot and steamy, furnished only with a tiled bench and hose. We stripped down and washed our bodies and hair, laughing and chatting and exchanging gossip, which is traditional at the baths. I was nervous when a woman appeared to wash us, a large-bosomed lady, naked except for tiny panties.

She rubbed us with a *kisseh*, a mitten of special canvaslike material, on which she put *sedr*, a rather grainy soap. This process removes the dry skin as well as the dirt. The same peeling and scraping can be done at home, but it's not as much fun; there's no laughter, no gossip, and no wet hair. A cabinet minister later told me he was always astonished at the amount of dirt that came off in the *hammam* when he thought he was so clean.

I loved it. Hours later we emerged feeling soft, beautiful, and magnificently clean. It was around five-thirty, when the bustle begins with renewed zest in Tehran. The streets and stores stay open and busy until eight-thirty.

My friend and I walked along the streets aware of the high walls and the murmuring of voices and the sound of the fountains that are in every garden. I could see the blue tiled minarets of a mosque in the distance and hear the *moezzin*—the call to prayers—in the distance. Bidding farewell to Marie, I wanted to see if I could get home in a taxi, always a risky business in a strange city as any visitor to New York, Washington, Paris, or Tehran will confirm. I tried to flag down a few and finally one stopped. But after arriving more or less near the embassy, I forgot to look at the meter. Chagrined, I paid what the driver demanded. The next day I squeezed in with three chadori women and looked at the meter, but the mountains were going the wrong way. The third time I put it all together, the direction, the meter, and a "ball park" fare, and I spent the evening basking in my sense of accomplishment.

My delight in getting around the city on my own was short-lived. In early June, Lewis Lee Hawkins, a lieutenant colonel attached to the American Military Assistance Group in Tehran, was assassinated. He had left his house early one morning to walk a short distance to the place where a car pool picked him up. In doing so, he ignored a cardinal rule of security—don't follow the same route at the same time every day. The terrorists were waiting for him. As he passed a *kucheh,* a small alley, gunfire struck him in the back, spinning him around. More bullets hit him in the chest, and he went down. Two men roared out of the *kucheh* on a motor bike and rushed away down the main street. Before help could reach him, Lieutenant Colonel Hawkins was dead.

The murder of Colonel Hawkins made me finally realize that Dick and the security officers were no longer talking about possibilities, but realities. Leaving the embassy compound, even with a guard, might have devastating results.

4

From Zoroaster to Mohammad

Do not step on a Persian carpet or a mullah because it increases their value.

Following the overthrow of the Shah in 1979 by a powerful religious leader, Americans and Europeans became aware of Iran as never before. Suddenly newspapers, magazines, and television programs were filled with information about this exotic, volatile country where religion plays such an enormous role. But it is still difficult for Westerners, who separate church and state, to understand Islam's all-pervasive effect in Iran. For a true believer, Moslem law governs all aspects of life.

As the Ayatollah Khomeini, the man who led the revolt against the Shah, said soon after his return to Iran, "From the beginning, Islam represented a political power, not limiting itself to problems of religious practice. In fact, if one refers to the practices of Mohammad, which are the main Moslem texts, one sees that they deal as much with politics, government, the struggle against tyrants, as with prayers. Our religion does not have strict rules regulating relations between man and God.

Just like a state does, our religion associates politics with social problems and prayers."

Political talk in Iran—in fact any serious discussion—is difficult to follow unless you have some comprehension of Shi'ite jurisprudence. This is basically an all-encompassing set of rules that governs the believers' relations with God and with their fellow men. The rules are taken from more than one source: the Koran, the *Hadith* or *Sonnat*, and *Ejma*, the concensus. Moslems consider the Koran the word of God as revealed to Mohammad. It may not be added to, but it may be reinterpreted. This has often led to strong differences of opinion among the religious scholars. The *Hadith*, or the Tradition, is comprised of sayings and examples of Mohammad. *Ejma*, or the concensus, is a rule agreed upon by all the religious jurisprudents. Moslems yearn to emulate the Prophet, and if the Koran does not provide guidance for a specific action, then direction is found in the *Hadith* or *Ejma*.

I often sat next to the Iranian Foreign Minister, Abbasali Khalatbary, during many long official dinners, and I found this quiet, shy, scholarly man always willing to answer my questions. (He was imprisoned during the revolution that overthrew the Shah and later shot, as were other members of the regime.) We continued our conversations from dinner to dinner, but the more he told me the more I realized that such a complex subject needed further study. I decided to sign up for classes under Seyyed Hossein Nasr, a Sufi scholar and a professor of Islamic philosophy at Tehran University. My first objective was to put Persian religions into historical perspective.

Many religions have left their mark on the culture of the country. Thirteen centuries ago Zoroastrianism was widespread in Iran. There is no agreement among the scholars about the date of Zoroaster's life. David Stronach, a British archeologist excavating at Tappeh Nush-e Jan, a Median period site in the province of Kermanshah, has found a mud brick fire altar dated about 730 B.C. This is the earliest fire temple discovered so far and fixes an earlier date for Zoroaster's life than the scholars had come to accept.

When I visited Stronach's camp, he told me that Zoroaster, a Mede himself, had to flee Media after facing strong opposition from priests of the local cults whom he had accused of being devil worshipers. Though locked in a power struggle with their Assyrian neighbors, the Medes were at that time the dominant power in western Iran. This was just prior to the founding of the Achaemenian Empire by Cyrus the Great.

At the age of twenty, Zoroaster withdrew from the world and spent ten years in meditation. He emerged to preach his new religion, at first with little success. In time a Persian king adopted his faith and Zoroastrianism became the official religion of the Achaemenian Empire.

Zoroastrians believe that the forces of good and evil are in constant struggle until in the end goodness becomes triumphant. Ahura Mazda is the source of all goodness, purity, and light, and Ahriman the source of all evil and darkness. The world is the stage for this important struggle. Zoroastrians lay great stress on angelic beings and believe that each species in this world is governed by an angel. The Persian months still bear the names of these angelic beings—guardians of both nature and man arrayed against the forces of Ahriman. Zoroastrians also believe in life after death, judgment of the soul, heaven and hell, resurrection, and the final day of judgment. Today there are only a few thousand Zoroastrians in Iran. They live for the most part around Yazd and the southern central city of Kerman, a place now known for its carpets and pistachios.

Soon after our arrival in Iran, Dick told me he was going to Kerman on embassy business. I asked one of the Iranians in the embassy if he

Yazd is one of the many Iranian towns I visited. In the foreground are domed peasant houses made of mud brick.

could find a way for us to visit the Zoroastrian center there. We were lucky. He knew one of the leading families of the church, and they agreed to see us. We drove down one afternoon and arrived in Kerman just at dusk.

By the year 1271, the time of Marco Polo's visit, Kerman had become an emporium for trade. A lovely desert town surrounded by high mountains, it has witnessed a lot of suffering throughout history. It was one of the last holdouts at the time of the Islamic conquest; in the eighteenth century Aqa Mohammad put thousands of Kermanis to death while blinding and sending into slavery thousands more for harboring the last of the Zands dynasty.

We stayed in a small inn near the mosque. The clear bright early morning sun awoke us, and we ate fresh *barbari* bread and cheese, and drank strong tea. Then we drove past the remains of the medieval city walls and the Sasanian and Seljuk monuments, catching glimpses of tall pine and cypress trees behind high garden walls.

The Zoroastrian family's two sons took us to their father's house, which we entered through large iron gates. Inside the high wall was a courtyard. Only a trickle of water ran from the central fountain, but the flowers bloomed in disorderly profusion. The surrounding family houses were cooled by the *badgir,* or wind tower, a chimney in reverse that ventilates rooms below ground level. The family made us feel welcome and while we were in their house showed us pictures of an American they had entertained before.

At last we reached the temple. In a Zoroastrian temple a fire burns continuously. Zoroastrians are not fire worshipers: The fire is a symbol of Ahura Mazda. The priest, dressed in long white robes, chanted from the Avesta, their sacred book. It is handwritten in the Avestan language, one of the oldest Indo-European languages in the world. Zoroastrians put great stress on purity, inward and outward, and emphasize the purity of the elements. So as not to defile the earth, they did not, until recently, bury their dead, but preferred to leave them on top of a hill in what are known as "towers of silence."

We drove through fields of pistachio trees to one of these towers which are now illegal for sanitary reasons. In the past, bodies were placed inside a circular wall near drainage channels. Rain would then wash the remains to a central drain. A few hundred yards away and down a hill a friend or a relative of the deceased waited for three days with a lighted lantern in the window of a building. The vigil would last until it was sure that life had left the loved one and that there was no call for help from the "tower of silence" above. Would the circling vultures be equally patient? I decided I wouldn't want to risk finding out.

The trip to Kerman stimulated me in my studies; I had problems only with trying to fit my classes into a growing diplomatic schedule and with my Iranian security guards, who were less than happy with my new student status. I wore inconspicuous clothes, and my guard always stayed some distance behind me, sitting on the other side of the room during classes in order not to attract attention. But students were demonstrating more and more often on the campus as their resentment against the Shah's regime grew, and as it was dark when Professor Nasr's lectures were over, the guards always drove me straight home.

Nevertheless, inside the classroom, my fellow classmates and I pursued our studies. The other students were mostly young Indians, Pakistanis, or Iranians who had been studying the mystical philosophy of Sufism for years, or young Americans working on their graduate degrees in some aspect of Iranian culture. We were discovering the philosophies

A "tower of silence" and, below, the building where relatives would wait to be sure there was no sign of life.

of the great Islamic teachers who had, perhaps, set the tone for the very state of mind that created the demonstrations outside.

We began, of course, with Mohammad. His name means "the praised," and he was born in Mecca in 570 A.D. to a family of the powerful Quraysh tribe. His father died before he was born. As was the custom at that time, his mother gave him to a wet nurse, a bedouin woman from the Benu Said tribe, known for speaking the purest Arabic. His mother died when he was in his sixth year, and he was raised by older relatives.

When Mohammad was born, Mecca was a bustling caravan city, the center of trade between India in the east and Petra and Gaza in the north. Mecca was also the site of Arabia's holiest shrine, the Kaaba, which in those days contained over three hundred idols for worship. Among them was Allah, the chief deity, creator of the universe. Many of the rituals carried out by the worshipers at that time are similar to those honored by the pilgrims of today.

After one journey with a caravan at the age of twelve, Mohammad spent the remainder of his youth as a shepherd. Not until he was twenty-five did he go to Syria, in charge of a caravan for Khadijeh, a wealthy widow and businesswoman whom he later married. Though she was fifteen years his senior, she bore him seven children. The three sons died and of the four daughters only Fatima, later married to Ali, his chosen successor, bore him descendants. Thus all descendants of Mohammad come through his daughter. (So much for the totally male-oriented society!)

Mohammad, on his trips with the caravan, doubtless listened to Jewish and Christian preachers, and after he married Khadijeh he spent more time in peace and quiet and contemplation. Every year Mohammad retired with his family for a month to a cave in the desert for meditation. His chosen month was Ramazan, and it was during Ramazan in his fortieth year that his first revelation came to him. (Now, each year during Ramazan, Moslems perform a month's fasting, called *ruzeh* in Persian.)

For the next thirteen years he encountered violent opposition to his preachings, which forced him to flee from Mecca to Yathrib, now known as Medina. With this *hijra,* or migration, in 622 A.D., the Moslem era was born and it is from that date that all Moslem countries begin their calendar. (For Moslems 1980 is 1400 by the lunar calendar; for the Iranians who use a solar calendar along with the religious lunar calendar it is 1358.) Mohammad, who had been known only as a preacher, became ruler of a state that grew in ten years to be the empire of Arabia.

During his lifetime the Prophet Mohammad united all of Arabia under Islam, a Semitic religion. Not until after his death did Islam spread outside Arabia. Conquering part of Byzantium, the Moslems, by now a strong unified force, succeeded against great numerical odds in conquering Persia, whose people were worn out by their struggle against the Byzantine Empire. This was by the middle of the seventh century.

The Moslems, however, permitted "People of the Book" (Jews, Christians, and Zoroastrians) to continue to practice their religions. So while a great majority became followers of Islam, the conversion was not complete.

After the death of Mohammad in 632 A.D. Islam spread rapidly. Living in sixty countries as far apart as Algeria, the Philippines, and China, the Islamic community is estimated at more than eight hundred million. The number is rapidly increasing, as the birth rate among Moslems is high.

Throughout their history the Persians have maintained a certain identity and independence; their spirit seems to be unconquerable. Even after the spread of Islam, they retained their culture and many of their earlier traditions, and though they became Moslem they gradually adopted a new branch of the Moslem faith called Shi'ism, after Shi'at Ali, "party of Ali." (The party of Ali has many different sects, but the two main ones are Isma'ilis, made world famous by their leader the Aga Khan, who believe in seven Imams, and those, by far the largest group, who believe in twelve Imams.) Since the great majority of Moslems in the world are Sunnis (after Sunna, the practices of the Prophet), this difference has tended to isolate Iranian Shi'ites from the Arab, or Sunni, Moslems. But more significant, it encouraged the individualism of a national, cohesive force in Iran.

It was not, however, until the time of the Safavids in the early sixteenth century that Shah Isma'il imported Shi'ite teachers from several Arab lands especially to help expand the religion, and Shi'ism became the state religion of Iran. Encouraged in Iran as the national religion to fight the Sunni Ottoman Turks in the seventeenth century, many believe it became more militant than the Sunni sect.

Shi'ites and Sunnis differ mainly on the question of the succession to the Prophet Mohammad and the function of the successor. The Sunnis believe that the Caliph (successor) should be selected by a consensus of the Moslem community or its representatives. The Shi'ites believe that the rightful succession to Mohammad is through the direct line of Fatima, his daughter, and his son-in-law and cousin, Ali. They believe Ali is the first Imam or divinely inspired leader. One of the reasons that the Persians emerged as the followers of Ali was the never-confirmed belief that the younger son of Ali and Fatima had married Shahrbanu, the daughter of the last king of the Sasanians.

At the heart of the Shi'ite doctrine is the importance given to the Imams. They are considered to be the appointed successors to the Prophet and are credited even in death with the power to heal or intercede on judgment day. In Iran about twenty-nine million out of a population of thirty-six million are duodecimal (twelver) Shi'ites. They believe Imam Ali was succeeded by eleven other Imams. The Shi'ites believe in the continuous existence of the twelfth Imam, who disappeared physically in the year 874 but is said to exist in spirit. This Imam will reappear on earth as the Mahdi to prepare for the second coming of Christ and will one day bring about justice and redemption to true believers. Until that time the community is led by *ulama,* who are considered to be vicars of the Mahdi.

Participating in the leadership of the eighty thousand Iranian mosques, or places of religious significance, are about one hundred eighty thousand mullahs, or religious teachers of all ranks. They range in no particular hierarchy from teachers who deliver lectures on the Koran and have little education to religious scholars who have completed courses in one or more of the three hundred theological schools. Each of these centers benefits from an eminent scholar, who usually has the title of Ayatollah, or "sign of Allah." Although this title is used fairly loosely, the more accurate title is Mujtahid, which means authority in the religious sciences and religious law. Each such person receives religious taxes and contributions. A Shi'ite may choose the Mujtahid whom he will follow, and can change allegiance any time he wishes. The popularity, prestige, and power of any Mujtahid can and does change. There are several well-known Mujtahids, usually called Grand Ayatollahs, all elderly and considered leaders of eminence because of their greater learning, wisdom, and piety. They emerge as leaders by consensus. Each one of these religious leaders has a book, *Ressaleh,* in which is set forth all the problems and answers. For example, should a driver in the service of a man who drinks alcoholic beverages quit or can he continue?

Traditionally, Shi'ite clergy do not create public opinion, rather they serve as a vehicle for expressing public opinion. But there is no doubt that at the time of revolution the mullahs play a great role in inciting the people and causing dissatisfaction, not in just reflecting it. It was to the mosque that the dissatisfied citizens went in the months before the late Shah's downfall, particularly as no other means of political expression had been developed.

The Constitution of 1906 introduced separation of executive, legislative, and judicial branches of the government. It also provided for the formation of a Parliament: the Majlis and the Senate, although the Senate was not convened for many years. The conservative clergy thought this separation of religion and state was not legal in religious terms and was too Western a concept, and the argument still exists between Islam and modern secular political practice.

This 1906 Constitution recognizes the Shi'a branch of Islam as the state religion, and the Shah, who ruled in the name of the twelfth Imam, had to promote Shi'a doctrines. According to this Constitution, a committee of five religious leaders had to pronounce that all Parliamentary legislation was in harmony with Islamic principles. Cabinet officials are required to be Moslem. Although there has been some limitation on the political activity of the minority religious groups, freedom of worship is guaranteed as a civil right. The Constitution recognizes Zoroastrianism, Judaism, and Christianity. Bahaism, a sect founded in Iran in the mid-nineteenth century and never recognized, is a community of about three hundred thousand people, but it has been contended that it is in fact a political group and through the years its members have been subjected to persecution.

There is one seat in the Majlis for the Zoroastrian community, one for the Jews, one for the Assyrian Christians, and two for the Armenians, of which there are now about one hundred fifty thousand in Iran.

Each month I spent in Iran I became more aware of the aspects of its religions that, though not immediately apparent, are a strong influence on the people.

The *zurkhaneh,* for instance, is traditional religious gymnastics performed by men who are chosen at the age of sixteen for their strength, physique, and moral character. Elsa Gibson, from Harvard, describes it this way:

Prayer and mystic—ancient Iranian heroes and weapons, music, epic and lyric poems, the splendor of Persian architecture and the delicacy of ethereal tiles, glittering mirrors and a dusty pit, gorgeous embroidered trousers and humility of the soul. Striving to perfect the body in order to offer it back to Allah, its source, all this is Zurkhaneh, the "House of Strength" an institution as old as Islam, a tradition of physical training in Iran still alive and as old as Persepolis.

We went many times to the House of Strength before we could begin to understand the traditional practice of physical fitness. The ultimate accomplishment is not a black belt, but to be a Pahlevan, a strong hero par excellence whose entrance is from then on heralded by the roll of drums and a chorus of acclaim.

Zurkhanehs are hard to find. They are hidden in alleys or behind mosques, reminding us that this tradition was discouraged and feared by foreign conquerors and even by Reza Shah, the first of the Pahlavis. But it was kept alive by the same independence that sustained Iranians during the occupation of their country by Arabs, Mongols, and Europeans through the centuries. Perhaps the tradition started with the Zoroastrian belief that, by virtue of physical strength, evil could be banished from the earth.

By now it began to dawn on me that I was never going to understand Iranians, even if I could clear my mind of Western thought and logic. The subtle nuances which had derived from cultural, religious, and political interplay dating back centuries were much more foreign to my Western mind than I had realized. Iranians do not think the way we do and I was beginning to understand this.

5

Unpaid Diplomat

One should not expect fruit from a willow tree.

An ambassador's wife is always on the job. Every
embassy is different and some are much busier than others. The Tehran
embassy was extremely active. When Dick decided to accept the post
in Iran, I never dreamed that I would work so hard or that it would be
"so daily," as the proverbial maid said about housework.

Like many other embassies, the residence and the chancery (embassy
offices) were in the same compound. The ambassador's office was in the
chancery along with the administrative, commercial, petroleum, and
agriculture offices. The political offices, the military attachés, the security group, and such support services as the mail office and the communications were also all in the main chancery buildings.

The consular section was in a large building in a nearby part of town
and was later moved to the embassy compound. The consul and his staff
were responsible for liaison with expatriation problems: Americans
married to Iranians, births, deaths, any American visitor's problems

with the police or the courts, or drug violations. They also issued visas to enter the United States.

Where does an ambassador's wife fit into all this? If the ambassador is the personal representative of the President, charged with carrying out his country's foreign policy, what does an ambassador's wife do?

Among other things, she is in charge of the residence. (When a single person is appointed ambassador, he or she might have a paid housekeeper appointed by the State Department and perhaps a relative to assist in entertaining.) In some small post this may include maintenance and repair as well as the supervision of residence staff.

Another major and traditional role is preparing for, and being hostess at, representational functions. The wife of an ambassador or a chargé d'affaires averages three nights out a week at official functions and the same entertaining officially at home. This doesn't count the time it takes "to keep hair done and change clothes."

The amount of time spent preparing for these functions varies, depending on the type of gathering, the ease of shopping at the post, the availability of household help, and the capabilities of that help. One ambassador's wife reported having to cross a large city to shop for things she needed for representational entertaining. At another post, the food supply is so bad that periodic automobile trips to a neighboring country are necessary to keep the embassy adequately supplied. These may be extreme cases, but a minimum of two hours preparation time was usual.

No secretary is provided for the ambassador's wife, although she can pay for one herself. Some ambassadors in particularly socially demanding posts such as those in Paris or London have negotiated with the State Department for more help than they are usually assigned, but this is an uncommon arrangement. We did have a social secretary who sent out invitations and kept the ambassador's schedule, but she was in no way obligated to help me keep my schedule or even to take messages for me.

There was no head housekeeper in the Tehran residence. I ran things myself, overseeing the servants and the housekeeping, ordering the meals, the food, and the household supplies. In Tehran, this all took much longer than I could ever have imagined at home. Living in an official residence, we were obliged to provide lodging for senior American government officials (the Tehran hotels were always full). This proved to be costly. If an official stays in a hotel, he receives a government reimbursement on a per diem basis; if an ambassador puts him up, then the *ambassador* pays for the food and the extra work by the servants. In a busy post with many exchanges between governments, or in a country attractive enough to entice a lot of visiting officials, having guests can add up to quite a large ambassadorial bill!

In order to run the Tehran residence in the most efficient way, I did the food shopping myself. Meals had to be arranged with whatever food was available. With the lack of refrigerated transportation, very little was brought to Tehran from the Persian Gulf. When we managed to find someone who could bring us a cooler full of fish, it was like opening a treasure trove. You never knew what you would find inside. Fish from the Caspian, such as sturgeon, was more readily available.

I could request from the government a refund for certain designated types of entertaining, but it was necessary to keep track of all food and liquor that came into the house—and what went out, which sometimes was more difficult. Few people drank milk, but our milk bill always seemed high. One month we used six hundred tea bags, although very few of our guests had tea. Farooq, the head butler, was meticulous about the liquor, which we kept under lock and key. As a good Moslem, he did not drink spirits and would not allow me to employ "tipplers" as extra help for parties.

It cost me twice as much to feed the servants as it did the guests. The Moslem servants did not like to eat American meat from the commissary; they wanted Iranian chickens, which are scrawny and expensive (they thought our chickens had no taste). Nor did they like American rice. The rice, which they ate every day, had to be bought on the local market. I bought it by the sack, but it would disappear like the melting snow, and I was tempted to sleep with it under the bed. Whatever system I tried, the bookkeeping was tedious and time-consuming.

Our first high-ranking official visitors were Secretary of State and Mrs. William Rogers, who were coming for a Central Treaty Organization (CENTO) meeting. I had heard the horror stories about VIP visits to embassies: aides taking over houses and staff, leaving them in a shambles; possessions, including silver, missing; kitchens turned into disaster areas; vicious dissension over the appropriateness of artwork hanging in the embassies. (You only need to scratch a State Department veteran to elicit such stories.)

I was therefore not unduly surprised one morning a few days before the Rogerses' arrival when an unknown American swept in through the front door clutching a plan of the residence. I happened to be in the entrance hall arranging flowers, and I introduced myself. He wasted no time going straight to the point. In stentorian tones he announced the earthshaking news that the Secretary would arrive in a few days to stay at the residence. As if we didn't know!

Then he said, "You will give him your bedroom."

I replied, "Certainly not."

He did not utter another word, but he seemed to clutch the floor plan a little tighter as he disappeared upstairs. I did not go on to explain that the VIP suite was really better furnished and in a quieter location than ours, and that we were being charged rent for our apartment. Were we to sublet to the Secretary?

Just before the Secretary arrived, Dick had his first diplomatic incident. We were out for dinner when Dick received a formal, urgent telephone call requesting his presence immediately at the home of the Iranian Foreign Minister. William Clements, Deputy Secretary of Defense, had made a speech in the United States suggesting the Persian Gulf be renamed the Persian-Arabian Gulf. As the Shah pointed out any time the subject came up, it is the Persian Gulf, it has always been so named, and it is so named on all ancient maps. Even on ancient Russian maps.

The Secretary was already airborne from his previous destination, but the Foreign Minister said that unless the U.S. government corrected or apologized for the suggestion, the Shah would find it impossible to receive the Secretary of State after he arrived. Dick was able to reach a Deputy Secretary of State in Washington, who issued a clarifying statement. The problem was corrected just in time, and the Secretary landed not knowing about the last-minute panic. The Shah later commented to the Secretary, "The weather is sometimes inclement in Washington."

Secretary and Mrs. Rogers had a special quiet charm that was appealing; they were delightful guests. During their visit Adele Rogers requested a meeting with the wives of foreign service officers and other members of the embassy who could be spared from their office work. Sitting on the floor surrounded by the wives, she discussed the problems of being abroad in an informal, morale-boosting coffee session. This type of meeting is particularly helpful when you are in difficult and different circumstances and can only hope that somebody high up wants to know your suggestions, thoughts, and struggles.

The Secretary's visit brought our first experience with a motorcade.

Something happens to ordinary drivers and escort police in motorcades. Do they act out sublimated fantasies? Does the power of their vehicles or their passengers go to their throttles?

At the airport Adele Rogers and I were assigned car number six. The first five cars were occupied by the Secretary, his Iranian counterpart, the Foreign Minister and Dick, protocol officers, and secret service and Iranian security guards. Our car was placed sixth in line away from the door of the VIP lounge. The red carpet leading from the door was as always auspiciously held in place by heavy gold-colored bricks. Before we could reach our car the lead car was off to a flying start. Trying to be gracious, leaping over gold bricks, I almost threw Adele into the car seconds before it shot off. With screaming sirens and lead-footed drivers who alternately applied brakes and accelerators, we hiccupped our way through congested streets to an embassy that seemed endless miles away. Every time the brakes were jammed on, Adele and I would try desperately not to end up on the floor. I had the advantage, as I had learned to sit braced in the back of any car. I tried to look nonchalant as she asked if it was always this way.

After this experience, every time we went to the airport to greet guests as they came down the ramp, I found myself evaluating their athletic ability and whether they could make car number six before the motorcade left. I often considered suggesting that they travel in tennis shoes, and I wondered what they thought about an ambassador's wife who stood in a takeoff position and whose eyes watched the cars lining up with a transfixed smile while she measured the "course."

They should be grateful that not once did I follow my natural instincts and yell at the top of my lungs, "Run." This exercise continued for three years and then, just as I had it down to a fine art, arrangements were made to use helicopters for transporting VIPs.

Motorcades were not the only way we greeted visitors. Some of the more adventurous friends passed through on a bus on their way to Katmandu, and one set of young people arrived in a station wagon en route to India. Visitors from the private sector, from universities or private traveling groups, were always coming through, and we found there were various ways to help them. Some had been traveling in the East and had loads of dirty laundry; others were mostly anxious to eat a plain meal.

When we received a congressional delegation—known in the trade as Codel—not only did wives usually need to be escorted, but often there were packages that had to be mailed after visits. One senator stayed at a local hotel as a guest of the Iranian government, but he wanted the remains of the nuts and the soap from his room mailed after he left.

We were surprised at how many members of Congress thought Iran was an Arab country. I often bet Dick that a visitor would say, "Now this *Arab* country . . ." I won a lot of quarters. We found that many of our other guests also thought of Iran as an Arab country. At one meeting with government officials Dick came back to the embassy looking pale. A U.S. senator had told a high-ranking Iranian he was sorry he wouldn't be able to visit with their chief of state, King Hussein!

Travelers who had come by plane were anxious to exercise. Tehran is a long way from America, six thousand miles, and with an eight-and-a-half-hour change in the time zones they needed something to bring them back to life. Dick and I were sneaky—we challenged our guests at tennis before they became used to the higher altitude.

After dinner I would show films to our guests, most of whom were Iranian or foreign diplomats, but this was troublesome when I borrowed films from American commercial film companies, because so many of them weren't suitable for an Islamic country. The stories they depicted were too permissive. I turned to Iranian films, and we met talented filmmakers, young and old, whose sensitive portrayal of their culture presented us with an ideal way to introduce our American visitors to Iran and to the Islamic religion. I found a unique film on the *hajj,* the pilgrimage to Mecca, made by hidden cameras. One other Iranian film I turned up elicited an interesting reaction. One night after dinner we showed a film taken in the mosque in Mashhad. This is the most venerated mosque in Iran for the Shi'ite Moslems and only recently have even a few Westerners been allowed inside or even in the environs. When the film was over a cabinet minister sitting beside me was obviously very moved.

"Cynthia, I'm glad you showed that film," he said. "We in Tehran are apt to forget the depth of feeling out there in the countryside." A very prescient remark.

We also met the International Iranian Bridge team, fresh from success in a tournament in Beirut. Cautiously, I asked one of the members if the team would be kind enough to come and teach us to play bridge. He said they would love it. It turned out that they had never been inside the American embassy.

A major concern for me was the morale of the other American wives.

The classic role for wives used to be taken for granted. They came to parties at the embassy to help entertain their counterparts in the host country. They would help with some of the necessary chores, such as finding volunteers to ride the school bus, take the wives of VIPs around when necessary, and they were, according to their husband's rank, to be responsible and concerned for the welfare of the wives junior to them or in their same section. Many wives enjoyed this participation, but it had been misused. Ordered to bring food for parties, ordered to do things for the ambassador's wife or the embassy, they felt these things were outside their responsibility. In 1972, in direct response to this growing belief that the Foreign Service should not expect to get two for the price of one, the director general of the Foreign Service issued a directive stating that the wives of Foreign Service officers were no longer required to perform duties as unpaid members of the Foreign Service.

This directive presumably also applied to the ambassador's wife. She was no longer responsible for the morale of the wives of the embassy officers.

But how could good morale in an embassy not be important? After all, we were all in it together. I found it impossible not to be at least interested and to try to help with their problems. A constant concern of mine was that we were unaware of some individual who desperately needed help. The heads of sections in the embassy are the ones who keep their eyes and ears open for this, but the adjustment for many was difficult. One family just installed in their new apartment was shattered to witness sheep being sacrificed on the balcony of the apartment next door. They had arrived on a religious festival and nobody had warned them.

I started a coffee morning once a month for the embassy wives. There were far too many military wives for me to include them all so I asked the wife of the senior officer in the country if she could devise a system to send a different group each month. I had not lived in a group where seniority was so important since my own naval days in England, but I was glad that I held firm and did not agree to have only the colonels' wives. The junior military wives seemed to enjoy these mornings more than anybody.

By now, even before we had finished all our calls, newer ambassadors were requesting to call on us. With temerity we changed the system and invited the couples to lunch. It seemed more humane, and it also left Dick and me free to exercise in that precious hour between the office

Relaxing at the pool in the rear of the embassy residence. (Ides van der Gracht)

and the evening rounds when we could enjoy a swim or a game of tennis. We established a tradition of tea alone in our apartment every evening before we went out. If we were going to survive the late dinners and long receptions ahead, we had to have time to ourselves. On our few free evenings we would read or listen to music. Dick, a conductor manqué, would conduct his favorite symphonies with a special baton donated by the director of the Tehran Symphony, Farhad Meskat, who had worked with Leonard Bernstein in New York.

Every day the embassy seemed busier than the day before. I was learning to live with my guards; by now we were used to their presence in the embassy. But one night we were giving a large dinner party and I was a little late going upstairs to change. I had stopped to check the tables and the seating arrangements. My husband, already changed, had gone downstairs ahead of me and was sitting in the drawing room. As was usual when we were entertaining, two of the servants were standing by the front door, one to let the guests in and the other to take their coats.

I came back downstairs about ten minutes before the first guests were expected. I walked into the room to find my husband talking to a woman I didn't know. A well-dressed woman of middle years, she was seated on the couch beside him. I sat down, expecting him to introduce me. She was not in evening clothes so I presumed she was there on business of some sort from the embassy. I looked at him quizzically; he was always polite, and yet he didn't introduce me. There was a strange silence and so I introduced myself. She looked very nervous and muttered something unintelligible.

I leaned closer to Dick and murmured, "Who is our guest?"

He whispered back, "I thought she must be a friend of yours. She just walked in through the front door."

The woman seemed more distraught. With growing horror I focused on her large handbag on the couch next to Dick. Where were our guards? I couldn't see them anywhere. As calmly as I could I suggested the woman come with me to an adjacent room, our library sitting room. Anything to get her away from my husband. I picked up her handbag and carried it for her, desperate to look inside, trying to decide how I could. We sat down on the couch in the library.

"How can I help you?" I asked.

"Madame Ambassador, I want to see you," she replied, speaking in Persian. "I must talk to you."

She began to mutter. I spoke to her again. Did she understand English? I tried Persian, but wasn't fluent enough. I lifted the intercom telephone. She didn't move. I was calling the chef, Luigi—his Persian was fluent. In the other room the guests, unknowing, were arriving and Dick was greeting them as though nothing were happening.

Where was the marine guard? Luigi was talking to the woman, keeping her occupied. I eased slowly across the room and picked up another phone. This time I reached the security office. It was all the way across the compound. I still had the woman's handbag; it seemed very heavy. I walked back to her and told her we were going upstairs.

Quite willingly she followed me away from all the guests, up to the sitting room of our apartment. We waited, Luigi and I taking turns talking to her until the marine walked at last into the room.

As I was going out of the door, he said, "Mrs. Helms, would you mind bringing my case upstairs?"

He had left his gun and his communicating equipment downstairs!

How had this strange event come to pass? Apparently, the woman was the disturbed wife of an Iranian judge, and years ago she had been the good friend of a previous ambassador's wife. She had walked to the

Dick and I greet members of the U.S. marine guard at the annual Marine Ball.

high outside wall on the east side of the embassy grounds and told a Tehran policeman on duty there that she wanted to see the ambassador's wife. He had taken her to the Iranian guard at the gate and told him that she had an appointment with me. As they both spoke the same language, this was an interesting interpretation of her request.

In spite of the fact that the guards were informed of every expected guest and they had no such information about this woman, the policeman brought her past the guards into the embassy and escorted her to the front door, which was open, because we were expecting dinner guests. When she walked in, the servants presumed she was one of the expected guests. The marine was not at his post and he probably would have assumed she had been checked at the gate anyway.

She walked straight into the house, on into the main reception room, and sat down beside my husband, probably the most guarded man in Iran besides the Shah.

Looking back at the incident, and other similar episodes, it seems to Dick and me that too much was expected of the marine guards at the age of eighteen or nineteen in handling the complexities of protecting our embassy and its occupants. It is our belief that in the future American embassies should be guarded by older and more highly trained individuals.

6

The Pahlavis: Father and Son

Knowledge acquired in childhood is like an inscription on stone.

Diplomats, politicians, and scholars may differ as to when modern Iran began, but 1925 seems to me to be the most accepted date. It was in that year that the late Shah's father, an almost illiterate army colonel named Reza Khan, was proclaimed Reza Shah after he had seized power in Tehran four years earlier. At the same time he also proclaimed his son, who was to go into exile fifty-four years later, Crown Prince Mohammad Reza.

The adoption of the name Pahlavi was significant. Pahlavi was an ancient Persian language with an awkward and cumbersome form of writing that disappeared after the Arab invasion in the seventh century. But the Persians eventually achieved their independence from the Arabic language, and Pahlavi reemerged as the language of today, although written in Arabic script and greatly enriched by many Arabic words.

Reza Shah's task in bringing Iran into the modern world was a formi-

dable one. For centuries the country had made little progress. Its people
included powerful tribes and various ethnic groups which didn't even
speak the same language or practice the same religious beliefs. Time and
again over the centuries Persia had been crisscrossed and overrun by
invading armies. More often than not, invaders appear to have been
culturally assimilated—witness the Chinese influence in Persian miniatures remaining after the Mongol occupation in the thirteenth century.
By and large, the Persians were able to retain a national identity of their
own.

Reza Shah, fiercely nationalistic and seeking to stir a feeling of national pride, recalled for his subjects two thousand years of Persian
history and reminded them that they did indeed have a glorious past—
Persia's magnificent golden age. He said they might recapture it again;
then he began the tremendous job of unifying his country.

One of his worst problems was the strong conglomerate tribal groups,
which were a threat to peaceful travel in their territories and had not
been subject to rule from Tehran. This was particularly true of the
Arabic-speaking area in southwest Iran where the Sheikh of Moham-
mareh, and not the authorities in Tehran, negotiated an agreement with
the British when they wanted to lay the first Anglo-Persian pipeline and
build a refinery at Abadan.

Reza Shah's job was made more difficult by his not-so-distant predecessors, who had made many concessions to foreign powers. In 1879
Naser od-Din Shah had allowed the Russians to form a brigade of
Persian Cossacks commanded by Russian officers in his country. This
stranglehold came about mainly through vast loans that Russia had
made to the Shah to pay for the extravagance of his court. Many other
concessions, economic and otherwise, were given to the Russians
throughout the latter part of the nineteenth century and the early part
of the twentieth.

British concessions and investments in Persia were also substantial.
The British East India Company, which began trading in the Persian
Gulf in the early seventeenth century, set up headquarters in the southern ports to facilitate not only the sea trade to India, but overland travel
to Shiraz and Esfahan, then the capital under Shah Abbas I.

Because Britain had no diplomatic representative in the country at
that time, the East India Company's power grew as it represented the
governor general of India to the court in Persia. As Denis Wright says
in his book, *The English Amongst the Persians,* Britain's primary interest in

Persia was "to maintain that country's independence and integrity as a vital element in the defense of the Indian Empire."

In the early years of the twentieth century, the Qajar dynasty, under Mozaffar od-Din Shah, spent tremendous sums of money, much of it borrowed from Russia, on trips to Europe, and members of the court amassed fortunes. As a result, there was no money in the treasury for rank and file officials to run the country, forcing the Iranian people themselves to form a constitutional group. The Shah was obliged to promise liberal reforms, and in August 1906 he proclaimed the Constitution, which provided for a Parliament with two chambers—the Majlis and the Senate. The Shah died the following January.

In 1907 Britain and Russia signed an agreement defining their respective roles in Afghanistan, Tibet, and Persia. Although they agreed to respect those countries' territorial independence, they nevertheless divided Persia into zones of influence, and both countries continued to interfere in all aspects of administration. This constant interference by foreign powers over the years is perhaps responsible for the ever-present conviction that nothing important happens in the country except as the result of a conspiracy. The ruling class particularly was prepared to believe that there was always some kind of conspiracy afoot. It might involve somebody outside the extended family, the local government, the Prime Minister, the Court, or more often some foreign power.

Mohammad Ali Shah (ruled 1907–1909) hated the restrictions of the Constitution and, anxious to restore absolute monarchy, turned once more to the Russians for support. The Russian commander of the Cossack Brigade unsuccessfully bombarded the Parliament building. Despite the Russian assistance, the Shah was unable to gain the support of the people. He was forced to flee to Russia and his eleven-year-old son was installed (with a regent) as Persia's ruler. The Russian troops remained in the northern part of the country. In 1911 the Iranian government engaged Morgan Shuster, an American attorney, and four American assistants to handle Iran's finances with full power, an arrangement Russia and Britain opposed. Shuster accomplished a great deal in not quite eight months, but a Russian ultimatum forced his departure. The Russians continued to extend their influence and occupied the northwest province of Iran.

During World War I Persia declared her neutrality, but Russia and Britain, and then the Germans and the Turks, were all active in the country. The Germans stirred up anti-British feelings among the Per-

sians and the nomadic tribes in southern Iran. To combat this the British
organized a force called South Persia Rifles, which was also capable of
defending India from a possible German invasion. When the Russian
Revolution took place in 1917 there were a large number of Russian
troops in northern Persia.

In 1878 Reza Khan was born in the isolated village of Alasht, high
in the Alborz Mountains. The rugged, independent people of Alasht,
proud of their pure Iranian ancestry, share this inaccessible part of their
country with the Assassins, the Isma'ili sect which broke away from the
Shi'a Moslems and settled in the remote, impregnable mountains. (If
you make the long trip by foot and by donkey, you can still see the
remains of their castles.) "Assassins," by the way, is a Western name.
It comes from a young member of the sect known as Hasan-e Sabbah.
During the time of the Seljuk dynasty in the eleventh century he gained
followers for his sect by drugging them in a secret garden with hashish.
He became the first Grand Master of the Assassins. It is from them the
Aga Khan, who now heads the sect, is descended.

Reza Khan's family had some military background. He was the
thirty-second child of Abbas Ali Khan, who had married his last wife
in Tehran just the year before. Reza Khan's father died when the child
was a few months old, and in the following spring his mother took him
on the long, arduous journey to Tehran. There he grew up, although he
was still totally illiterate when he joined the army at the age of fourteen.
(The degree of his subsequent literacy has never been established. It is
more than likely that he did learn to read and write. And quite naturally
the late Shah was anxious to prove that his father did not remain
illiterate.)

In late 1920 the British decided to withdraw their troops from Iran.
The decision was made for economic reasons and because an agreement
engineered by Lord Curzon, the British Foreign Secretary, providing
British assistance in numerous civil and military affairs of state had not
been ratified by the Majlis. By this time the Persians were heartily sick
of British and Russian interference in their affairs. But in 1921 they
signed the Treaty of Friendship with the Soviet Union in Moscow, a
treaty that still stands.

Major General Sir Edmund Ironsides was the British general in charge
at the time of Great Britain's withdrawal. In his diaries of that time, he
described the sad state of the whole Persian army and emphasized that

only the troops under Reza Khan, who by then was an officer in the Cossacks, had any semblance of order.

Ironsides, nervous about what the Bolsheviks would do after the British withdrawal, persuaded Ahmed Shah to replace Russian officers with Iranians. An Iranian political figure from Tehran was appointed commander of the Persian Cossacks, but he proved ineffectual, and Reza Khan, by than a colonel, was in effect in command. In early February 1921, after reorganizing and outfitting the troops, Ironsides visited them in Qazvin and put Reza Khan officially in charge. He extracted two commitments from Reza Khan: that he would not harm the British as they left and that the Shah would not be deposed. Although General Ironsides's diaries were published in book form while we were in Tehran, they were banned from the country. Was it because of the commitment not to depose the Shah?

On February 18 Ironsides left Persia, and two days later Reza Khan rallied his reequipped troops. After swearing allegiance to him, they marched on Tehran. They were tired of their ineffectual government. There was little opposition and Ahmed Shah prudently appointed Reza Khan head of the armed forces. Soon after he became Minister of War and in 1923 he was named Prime Minister. Not until 1925 was Ahmed Shah, by then living abroad, deposed by the Majlis, and the Qajar dynasty ended. The Majlis declared Reza Khan the new Shah in December 1925, and in April of the following year, in Golestan Palace, he was crowned Shahanshah (king of kings) of Persia.

His contemporaries say Reza Khan was an aloof man, unusually tall and strong, but of little personal charm. Still, he understood his own people, and he was not above joining his countrymen in a little intrigue and manipulation. Two of my friends, now well into their eighties, who knew him well, say he wanted Iran to attain greatness while putting an end to foreign economic and military influence. His goal was to return Persia to the Persians.

His first move was to bring law and order to the entire country. Brigands and tribal warfare made travel difficult and dangerous. Without a strong central government no other reforms could be carried out. Iran needed roads, and one of the Reza Shah's greatest achievements was the Trans-Iranian Railway.

He was careful not to touch the 1906 Constitution, but he saw he would have to reorganize the judicial system. The laws were still the religious laws of the Shi'ites, still carried out by the religious leaders, adequate at one time but not always appropriate for contemporary needs. In 1925, education, health care, and even a simple hygiene were minimal. Industry was nonexistent. Wheeled carts were possible on only three minor roads in the whole country. Pack animals were the only other form of transportation.

Slowly he created a central administration. He established schools and sent students abroad to study, convinced that only through education would the country become a strong, independent power. He wanted to eliminate and change the narrow and restrictive outlook of the mullahs, the religious leaders of Islam in Iran. But he wasn't able to finish what he started.

During the Second World War, the British and the Russians once again occupied the country. After the German attack on Russia in 1941, the British wanted to send military supplies across Iran to support Russia. But Reza Shah resisted drawing the country into the war this way and refused to eject the German technicians brought in to build factories and railroads. The British and Russians felt he was generally pro-German, and as his son said, "He was exiled by mutual consent."

On September 28, 1941, after calling on his people to give allegiance to his son and heir, Reza Shah sailed from southern Persia on a ship provided by the British with his fourth wife and eight of his ten children. The Crown Prince, his mother, and his twin sister, Princess Ashraf, stayed behind. Reza Khan died in Johannesburg, South Africa, in 1944.

Mohammad Reza Pahlavi, the new Shahanshah, was close to twenty-two years old when he succeeded to the Peacock throne, but he was prepared. All aspects of his education—first at Le Rosey in Switzerland, then at the military college in Iran—had been followed closely by Reza Shah, including his participation in sports. In Switzerland he had been allowed to play ice hockey, but not to ski. (The Court Minister, Assadollah Alam, who was the Shah's classmate at the military college, suggested to Dick and me that this was probably because Reza Shah thought skiing was dangerous; he didn't know that ice hockey was also rigorous.)

The Shah once noted that his special friend in childhood had been a boy named Hossein Fardoust, who accompanied him to school in Switzerland. Later Fardoust became an instructor at the military academy that the Shah attended. He went on to serve in many official capacities, ending up as Inspector General of the Court.

The Shah had great regard for his father, who had taken over at a time when Iran was in chaos. Reza Shah had pulled the country together, and for a time had dramatically reduced the foreign influences that had corrupted government officials at all levels. He also started Iran on the road to modernization, which, in the end, had much to do with his son's downfall.

Considered at first a rather weak and indecisive young man, the Shah spent much of his first years enjoying the pleasures of monarchy. The first major issues he faced were succession to the throne, the Russian presence in the province of Azarbayjan, and oil. By 1946, Iran's resentment of foreign domination applied particularly to oil. At a time when Iran was the world's largest oil exporter, the Anglo-Iranian Oil Company (AIOC) refused to increase royalties. A member of Parliament named Dr. Mohammad Mosaddeq became a prime mover of the law to nationalize oil, but negotiations over a two-year period led nowhere. In 1951, the situation exploded. A Prime Minister perceived to be pro-British was assassinated, a law authorizing nationalization and expropriation of AIOC was passed, and Mosaddeq was named Prime Minister. He was charged with implementing the nationalization law.

Although the Communist Tudeh party was outlawed in 1946 after an attempted assassination of the Shah, Mosaddeq rose to power as the leader of a broadly based coalition called the National Front. Its cement was hatred of the British. At this time the Shah and Mosaddeq were in agreement, however wary of each other they might have been. The period was short. Mosaddeq was related to the Qajars, whose dynasty had been ended by Reza Shah. There is little doubt that he intended, eventually, to do to Mohammad Reza Pahlavi what the latter's father had done to the Qajars, and very soon the Shah replaced the British as Mosaddeq's target. Mosaddeq rejected the mediation of the United States, whose leaders tried to intervene on behalf of the West, and in 1952 Mosaddeq broke relations with the British. (There is a very revealing chapter in *Silent Missions,* a book written by General Vernon Walters. He tells a story about Governor Averell Harriman trying to negotiate with Mosaddeq, with Dick Walters as interpreter. It is revealing because it shows how difficult negotiations can be with Iranians who don't intend to negotiate. By the end of each day there would be signs of progress, and each morning Mosaddeq would approach the negotiations as if nothing had happened the day before.)

Increasingly the struggle turned inward between the Shah and his

Prime Minister. In a test of strength Mosaddeq suddenly resigned. His successor lasted four days, turbulence ensued, and the Shah was forced to reappoint Mosaddeq, who appeared to be winning the struggle for power.

Meanwhile, the United States, concerned over the political and economic instability of a country so strategically located, became increasingly receptive to British views on Mosaddeq. A joint plan was conceived by the American and British governments to support the Shah in exercising his authority in the area of appointing Prime Ministers. He dismissed Mosaddeq and appointed General Fazlollah Zahedi. Mosaddeq arrested the bearer of his dismissal notice as well as others, accusing them of attempting a coup.

The Shah fled. Accompanied by Queen Sorayya, he flew in his own plane to Baghdad, where the Iranian ambassador, according to the Shah's story, tried to arrest him. In Tehran for the next two days there were demonstrations led by the outlawed Tudeh party, with Communist followers shouting "Death to the Shah!" Then the tide turned. Galvanized by the Central Intelligence Agency, the pro-Shah supporters from the bazaar and south Tehran, including the strongmen of the *zurkhaneh,* streamed forth to the cry of "Long Live the Shah!" The Shah's departure had forced the people to focus in on the activities of the Communists in support of Mosaddeq.

Mosaddeq was arrested and underwent a long trial. The Shah was welcomed back by cheering crowds. To help his ailing treasury, a new foreign oil consortium was worked out with Royal Dutch Shell, the French Petroleum Company (CFP), five major United States oil corporations, and a group of smaller American companies; the British retained a forty-percent share.

It was not until 1963, however, that the Shah gained enough support to begin his reforms. During his so-called White Revolution, later renamed the Shah-People Revolution, his plans, particularly the vote for women and the much-needed land reform, were often adamantly opposed by the people and the clergy. On January 22, 1963, four days before the referendum on these two issues, the religious leaders organized a violent demonstration against female participation in the election. Because of this opposition, it was announced on the radio that morning that women would be allowed to vote but only in separate ballot boxes that would not be tallied.

Street mobs made a particular effort to frighten the women, but the

Shah held firm. The petite wife of one of his ministers also held firm. When armed mobs of rioters charged down the street toward her house, Mrs. Alam, wife of the Prime Minister, called her husband's office to ask for reinforcements. When he informed her that he was unable to come, or to send help, Mrs. Alam, a crack shot, took a rifle onto the roof and in full view she calmly awaited the demonstrators. She was not harmed. This was an example of the determination of some women to participate in the affairs of the nation. In spite of all the efforts to intimidate women voters, six women were elected to the Majlis and two to the Senate.

The land reforms were more complex. Land was taken away from large landowners, which included both lay people, who often owned huge tracts with dozens of villages, and the clergy. The clergy, particularly an Ayatollah named Khomeini, violently opposed land reform. Over time, however, reduction in the ostentatious wealth of the mullahs was achieved in the public's eye. They now had the power of poverty.

One of the Shah's main thrusts was education. In 1956 literacy among the rural women was about one percent, and perhaps only as high as twenty percent among urban women. By 1972 the literacy rate had risen to thirty-one percent. One teacher told me it was hard for the children to learn to read and write. There is no printing in the Persian language, so they had to start with cursive writing. Initial learning was also very difficult, since the stories about the Shah that students had to learn required flowery language and difficult tenses.

Before there were schools, the clergy had been the main influence in all the people's lives; the people's only education was religious instruction, which had not included learning to read. This meant the religious leaders had the capacity to wield great influence over the whole population. Now they had to contend with state schools and universities. It should be noted that the Shah's government never reminded anyone that under a 1907 constitutional amendment a committee of five theologians should have the right to pronounce on the religious validity of laws passed by the Parliament.

With the Shah's reforms under way, the clergy fought back. In 1962 the Ayatollah Khomeini issued strong public statements against the vote for women, stating that it was contrary to their station in Islam. In 1963 he publicly fought land reform. His opposition to both of these issues undoubtedly gave the Ayatollah considerable support. His picture was displayed in the bazaars as one of the leaders of the opposition. There were riots in some of the cities, but an understanding was eventually reached with the authorities that the religious leaders would no longer oppose the state. Khomeini, however, later denounced these understandings. Even at that time he was making anti-American speeches. Finally, after continued dissension, he was exiled on November 4, 1964, briefly to Turkey, and then to Iraq, where he remained for fourteen years until forced in 1978 to move to France.

In spite of these clashes with the mullahs, the Shah worked to modernize a very backward country, and indeed he achieved results. By 1968, the per-capita income had risen to such an extent that Iran moved out of the group of least-developed countries. Although two-thirds of the country's thirty million people still lived in villages, the Shah had built a nationwide communications system, new roads, and bustling big cities. He was preoccupied with bringing reform to his country, and his ministers were required to report directly to him. He had an inspectorate attached to the Court, his own special bureau of close advisers, and Savak, the security service that has often been denounced both inside and outside of Iran.

The Shah was one of the few chiefs of state who saw ambassadors and other officials alone. He appeared sure of himself and had an excellent memory for facts that interested him. In the late 1960s Dean Rusk, then the U.S. Secretary of State, referred to the Shah as the best-informed man in the world, with the possible exception of the United States President. He pumped people who called on him for information, asked questions on state visits, and read voraciously both Iranian and foreign publications. To bring his country into the modern world, he had to work long hours, as did his wife, the Empress Farah Diba.

The Shah had married for the first time at nineteen, an "arranged" match with Princess Fawzia of Egypt. They had not met before the week of the wedding. In 1940 Fawzia gave birth to Princess Shahnaz. She returned to Egypt on an extended stay and eventually they were divorced.

Next the Shah married Sorayya Esfandiari, the daughter of a German mother and a Bakhtiyari tribesman. Sorayya could have no children, and since under the Persian Constitution the crown must pass by direct line to a male heir, the Shah decided in 1958 to marry again, even though he had been content with Sorayya.

His third wife was Farah Diba, whose father was an Iranian military man who died when she was nine years old. An only child, she was raised by her mother. Educated in Tehran at Italian and French schools, she continued her art studies in Paris for two years at the Ecole Speciale d'Architecture. For some time she was completely French-oriented, but she eventually turned her attention to her own culture.

Ardeshir Zahedi, the son of General Zahedi and later ambassador to the United States, introduced her to the Shah. Zahedi was then married to Princess Shahnaz and was working with Iranian students who were living abroad. Farah Diba came to see him to ask that the government ease financial restrictions on students studying in other countries. He was so impressed by her articulate and eloquent presentation that he and Princess Shahnaz together persuaded the Shah to meet her.

Farah Diba always teased the Shah about their first meeting. She told me they met in Paris at a reception for Persian students, but he didn't remember her. Nobody ever said whether she won her case on the student restrictions, but she married the Shah on December 21, 1959. In October 1960 she gave birth to the Crown Prince, the first of four children. The Shah delayed their Majesties' coronation until 1967; he wanted to wait until his country's progress was more secure.

When she married at twenty-one, the Empress was a shy, unsophisticated young woman. But she steadily developed an extraordinary ability to move between international figures and her own country's people. She went everywhere in Iran, not just where she was programmed to visit, talking with people of all classes. She had lunch with lepers because her attention would help get them accepted back into society. Her visits abroad were not just state protocol visits; she looked, listened, and learned.

Although she usually wore European couturier clothes, she began to promote local silk and cotton handprinted materials, particularly when she was traveling within the country. When she went abroad, she often wore dresses adorned with the beautiful embroidery of the Baluchi tribes in southeast Iran. As the royal couple became more appreciative and aware of their own culture, more and more evidence of it gradually appeared in their palaces. Beautiful pottery and many ancient artifacts were on display.

In the early 1960s Prime Minister Assadollah Alam asked the Israeli government to help devise a plan to develop tourism in Iran. Teddy Kollek, chairman of the Israeli Government Tourist Corporation and later the mayor of Jerusalem, headed the planning mission. Kollek recommended that when hotels, new roads, and modern transportation had been built at Persepolis, Iran should stage a big event to attract foreigners to these new tourist facilities. Little did he realize, he later admitted, that the extravaganza celebrating the twenty-five hundredth

THE OFFICIAL VISIT
Of

Their Imperial Majesties
MOHAMMAD REZA PAHLAVI ARYAMEHR
SHAHANSHAH OF IRAN

and

FARAH PAHLAVI
SHAHBANOU OF IRAN
To The

UNITED STATES OF AMERICA
May.1975

During their State visit to Washington in 1975, the Shah and Shabanu signed this memento for us.

anniversary of the founding of the Persian Empire would be that event.

It was in 1971, 2510 years after Cyrus the Great captured Babylon on October 12, 539 B.C., that the Shah held his famous two-week celebration near the ruins of Persepolis. One hundred and sixty desert acres were covered with some seventy tents, sumptuously decorated by Jansen's of Paris with French crystal, china, and linens, and hung with red silk and velvet and glittering chandeliers. Five hundred guests from sixty-nine countries, including nine kings, five queens, sixteen presidents, and three premiers, attended three days of royal festivities. A parade celebrated the country's dynasties, with Iranian soldiers in authentic Achaemenian, Sasanian, Parthian, and Safavid costume. The royal Court had new uniforms designed by Lanvin, and stitched with nearly one mile of gold thread. Chefs from Maxim's prepared a grand dinner of crayfish mousse, roast peacock stuffed with fois gras, champagne sherbet, and expensive French wine. Only the caviar used to stuff the quail eggs was Iranian.

The celebration was criticized by Iranians for its excessive cost—reportedly one hundred million dollars—and for its emphasis on French, rather than Iranian, food and decoration. Many viewed it, too, as a celebration of the Shah and his family, rather than the Iranian nation. Nevertheless, the tourist facilities built for the celebration became an important part of the national economy. If the celebration represented only the Pahlavi vision of Iran—a country with a glorious ancient history, able to partake in the amenities of the West—it was at least a vision which made Iran a participant in the modern world.

The Shah officially opened his celebration with a visit to the tomb of Cyrus the Great at Pasargadae. He prayed to the ancient king:

O Cyrus, great King, King of Kings, Achaemenian King, King of the land of Iran. I, the Shahanshah of Iran, offer thee salutations from myself and from my nation. Rest in peace, for we are awake, and we will always stay awake.

Just as the Shah finished, a desert wind arose suddenly, blowing sand over the onlookers. Such a wind was thought to be a good omen. It wasn't.

7

Journey into
the Past

*A wise man does not extinguish the fire and leave
the embers.*

Most Americans and Europeans, even those who
have received an expensive education, know little of the ancient history
of the Middle East. It is only in recent years, with the concern over oil
and the establishment of Israel after World War II, that we have become
curious about the region. Now, with the downfall of the Shah and the
taking of American hostages in the American embassy, our curiosity
over Iran has increased enormously.

From time to time, as the ambassador's wife, I had an opportunity to
travel outside Tehran and learn about Iran's past. One such opportunity
developed as a result of meeting a French archeologist, Jean Perrot. He
and his team had uncovered the statue of Darius I, a great Persian king
known to most Western students mainly because his military forces
were defeated by the Greeks at the famous battle of Marathon in
490 B.C.

Perrot's discovery was made at Susa, a town in the province of

Khuzestan, southeast of the famous old Babylonian and Mesopotamian areas. It was in Susa, in southwestern Iran, that the Persian Empire was born. Perrot had suggested we come and see the statue before it was moved. Dick needed to go south to check on developments in the agrobusiness area, and we decided to combine the trip with exploring the area where Persia's golden age had thrived and died.

On the flight down I found myself trying to recollect my school days. Like most of us, I had been taught about the early Greek and Roman empires; but who were the Medes and the Persians? Most of what is known to us about the Persians comes down to us from their contemporaries, the Greek historians, especially Herodotus, who was actually born in a town under Persian domination.

Archeologists have traced mud village settlements at the foot of the mountains of Khuzestan as early as the eighth millennium B.C. Evidence of a large artificial terrace found at Susa precedes the pyramids of Egypt by one thousand years. It is the oldest large terrace that has been found in the world.

From the earliest period excavated there, beautiful pottery has been found. Potters of that prehistoric period created, with the help of the newly invented potters wheel, the most elegant pieces, many of them painted with highly stylized birds and animals.

When we arrived at Susa, Perrot picked us up in his jeep and, speaking alternately in broken English and rapid-fire French (at times it was hard to tell the difference), he raced us around remains of the old palaces and the acropolis to see his great find in its original position. The area where it was uncovered had been worked on repeatedly, but Perrot and his team had decided, on a hunch, to continue in the same area. On the second day of their new season they had uncovered, buried in the sand, the clenched hand and forearm of what was obviously part of a large statue. They knew it was Darius as soon as they read the first cuneiform inscription. As they continued excavations in the vicinity of the sculpture, they gradually uncovered parts of the king's gate and the apadana, landmarks that had been historically documented but never found. They knew that the king's gate and the apadana had been built in Darius's time and had probably been covered with sand for centuries.

The inscriptions on the statue proved to be in four languages—Old Persian, Elamite, Akkadian, and Egyptian. It looked as if it was carved in limestone from the nearby Zagros Mountains, which had also been used in Persepolis and in the buildings at Susa. By the time we saw it, a team of scholars had read all the inscriptions, which said quite clearly that the statue "was the likeness of Darius and made on his orders."

The scholars were puzzled, however, by a part of the text that claimed it had been made in Egypt. Was it made by Egyptian workmen in Susa? The Egyptian influence and workmanship were evident. Or could it have possibly been sculpted in Egypt and shipped to Susa? Eventually the specialists decided the statue had indeed been made in Egypt. An analysis of the stone proved it to be sandstone, not from the Zagros but probably from Wadi Hamamet in Egypt, where another famous statue had been made, the one Darius erected along his canal between the Nile and the Red Sea. The sculpture must have been shipped via the Red Sea and the Persian Gulf to Susa.

Perrot took extraordinary care in uncovering it. As we drove up, he and his team were placing scaffolding around the base and were almost ready to move it. At the time, Perrot was still searching for the head, but no trace was found. The statue, beautifully sculpted in flowing robes, was eight feet tall and must originally have been about a foot taller.

The three cuneiform inscriptions intrigued Dick and me. George Cameron, a specialist in Near Eastern languages from the University of Michigan, explained to us later that Akkadian is the better-known Babylonian-Assyrian language. The Akkadian period began as early as 2340 B.C. In Elam, of which Susa was the capital, inscriptions in Elamite were placed alongside Akkadian inscriptions at about the same time.

Perrot said that we have come to think of Persia as the old, romantic name and Iran the modern country, but archeologists and historians have another explanation. Three thousand years ago the Aryans, a group of tribes of Indo-European origin, swept down from the north to the central plateau in two separate waves. They called their territory Iran, "land of the Aryans."

Long dominated by the Assyrians and Urartians, two of the tribes— the Medes and the Persians—gradually grew more powerful. Finally asserting themselves over their enemies, the Medes began building their own empire, with their capital at Ecbatana, which lies directly under modern-day Hamadan. Not until about 700 B.C. did the Persians move south, approaching Parsa from the north and then pushing westward to the plains of Khuzestan and the declining glory of the kingdom of Elam.

Cyrus, a member of the Achaemenid clan, overthrew the Median ruler, Astyges, and so brought fame and power to the province of Pars when he built his capital there. As the fame of the Achaemenians spread, the people of other countries came to know the land by the name of the one province of Pars and so the name Persia came about. As there is no letter *p* in Arabic, this province became Fars after the Islamic invasion, but the Zoroastrians who fled to India have retained the name of Parsees.

The Persian Empire, created over a relatively short period—seventy years—was founded by Cyrus the Great, the first of the Achaemenians (550–330 B.C.). Cyrus, probably the son of a minor Persian king, a vassal of the Medes, was a physically attractive and appealing man. He was also a man of extraordinarily exemplary character. Believing no man was fit to rule unless he was more capable than his subjects, he did not fall a victim to luxury and self-indulgence.

In 550 or 549 B.C. Cyrus united the Medes and the Persians by defeating Astyges the Mede, his grandfather, at Pasargadae. After the defeat he constructed a palace there.

We know that Cyrus made Ecbatana his summer residence, while Susa remained his winter capital. The court, all their followers, their goods and chattel, would spend the summer in Ecbatana, then return

The tomb of Cyrus the Great at Pasargadae where the Shah and many others paid homage. (IDES VAN DER GRACHT)

eight hundred miles south to Pasargadae (his capital and later the site of his tomb) and travel five hundred miles west to Susa for the winter. The center of government became wherever Cyrus was in residence. It is hard to imagine the problems of moving the camping equipment, feeding the people and animals, covering long distances through the mountain passes, and crossing the desert areas in the south. Even today we would find that a difficult journey, but they were traveling by foot, or on oxen, camel, mule, or horse. (Travel by horse has been well documented since 1800 B.C.)

Cyrus defeated Croessus in 547 B.C. and so added Lydia, in present-day Turkey, to the Persian Empire. It was on the plain before the battle of Sardis where the sight and stench of the camels in the Persian force put the Lydian war horses to flight. Cyrus's empire was extended still further to Babylonia, Syria, Phoenicia, and Palestine. After gaining control of much of eastern Iran later in 529, Babylon was conquered without a battle. It was here that, according to biblical sources, Cyrus showed great tolerance toward the Jews and allowed them to rebuild their temples and to return to their homeland, Jerusalem.

Cyrus's son, Cambyses, extended the empire to Egypt when he defeated Psamatik III at Pelusium in 525 B.C. Thus, the rulers of the Medes and the Persians also became pharaohs of Egypt.

When Cambyses died, he left no heir. Darius, who may have been a distant cousin of Cyrus, succeeded him. (It is often said that he was Zoroastrian, but the dispute over his religion continues. He did worship the god Ahura Mazda, but that would not necessarily make him a Zoroastrian. The name simply means wise, *Mazda,* lord, *Ahura.*) The story of how he won the election goes something like this: Seven contenders agreed amongst themselves to meet. The successor to Cambyses would be the one whose horse neighed first. Darius had a more imaginative groom than his six competitors.

Darius became disenchanted with Pasargadae and built Persepolis, the architectural glory of the Achaemenid kings. Called Parsa in the days of Darius, it was probably used as a ceremonial capital.

Persepolis must have been an extraordinary place. Aeschylus mistranslated the "city of Persians" as Persepolis, "the destroyer of cities," a misnomer which still persists. Built in splendid isolation on the plain of Marv Dasht at 5800 feet above the Persian Gulf, it is constructed of the gray limestone of the area. Unfortunately, this limestone is weathering badly on the excavated remains. Surpris-

A relief of a Persian *(left)* and a Mede at Persepolis. (PETER BELIN)

ingly, there is no evidence of any structure used purely for religious purposes. R. T. Hallock, an American historian, translated many of the seven to eight thousand cuneiform tablets that have survived, although he himself never visited Persepolis. The Elamite texts record many kinds of transfer of food products in the area around Persepolis and Susa, and the disbursement of silver from the Persepolis treasury. The texts mention that men, women, boys, girls, and women chiefs of work groups received equal rations with the male "chiefs." Some received thirty quarts of wine or fifty quarts of grain and from the treasury texts it is evident that some were paid in shekels, which represent strict equivalents. One shekel equaled ten quarts of wine, three shekels equaled one sheep, and so forth. Payment was probably made in silver when commodities were scarce, but all the workers were paid. Apparently women were paid equally, with one exception—mothers who had sons received ten quarts of wine or beer or sometimes twenty quarts of flour or cereal, while those who bore girls got only half as much.

Not much is known about Darius personally. He refounded the empire, which reached throughout the known world and across some of the unknown all the way to the Indus Valley. He sustained it through a time of much unrest. His subjects believed Darius enjoyed divine protection. He was recognized as a better administrator than Cyrus, building the great canal between the Nile and the Red Sea and overhauling the structure of taxation throughout the empire. Both silver and gold currency were coined during Darius's reign. The daric, a kind of medallion of pure gold weighing 130 grams, was used mostly for bribing the Greeks.

Darius placed throughout the empire his own representatives, who reported to him personally through a series of mounted couriers. He built the Royal Road, extending fifteen hundred miles from Sardis to Susa, to stay in communication with those he ruled. There were resting places where messengers spent the night and fresh horses were available at posting stations. Parts of this Royal Road are still visible. How could Darius possibly do it all? The answer is, he couldn't. The empire declined. By the time of the battle of Marathon in 490 B.C., the Persian Empire stretched from the Nile to Thrace, and on one occasion even to the Danube, and east to the Indus. Darius saw the battle, rightly, as a setback to a hitherto successful steady frontier advance. It was one of the great turning points in history.

High on the side of a mountain known as Bisitun (*Baga-stana,* Place of God)—322 feet above Iran's main east-west highway from Ecbatana and the highlands of Medea and Persia to the lowlands of Babylonia— the story of Darius, his conquests, his ascent to the throne, and the virtue of his god, Ahura Mazda, are recorded. A pictorial relief portrays Darius, his god, his bodyguards, and ten of his most bitter enemies. The story is written in cuneiform in three different languages of the times.

We drove north from Susa across the plains and flat agricultural land to Kermanshah, where we turned east hoping to see the carvings stand out. We traveled slowly, for none of the Iranians with us knew what we were looking for. I sat in the front seat holding a book and trying to follow the landmarks and the vague directions which we had been given. The carvings were so high on the mountains that at first we didn't see them and drove past. Then we stopped at a *chaykhaneh,* a tea house, and discovered we had gone too far. We had to turn back to the long narrow range of massive limestone crags and there, on the last peak towering over the valley, the Royal Road passing at its foot, was Bisitun, the mountain of the gods.

The ancients must have passed this way over many seasons, and there on the Royal Road you could sense Darius's search for a place to immortalize himself. He may have seen this crag, and perhaps noticing a nearby spring of pure water—the symbol of blessing and fertility—he chose this place, and then planned how he could be certain that the monument would be left intact by all who followed him. Giving no special status to his own mother tongue, he recorded his story in the three languages of the realm. Perhaps he believed that, in this way, all people would be able to read it. What he couldn't know was this carving, later to become as famous as the Rosetta Stone, would provide a key to scholars' attempts to decipher the three languages: Old Persian, Elamite, and Akkadian. It would also enable them to decipher documents found at Nineveh, Babylon, and Ur of the Chaldees.

In the nineteenth century a German, George Grotefeld, partly deciphered the inscriptions. But as Professor Cameron told me, much of the credit goes to Major General Henry C. Rawlinson—a British officer in the service of Shah Mohammad of the Qajar dynasty—who risked his life on a scaffolding hundreds of feet up the mountain to copy most of the cuneiform texts between 1835–47 and himself became a pioneer in the decipherment of the cuneiform. Cameron arrived in 1948 to complete the job. He hung on the side of the mountain on an ordinary painter's scaffold slung from steel wire and ropes. All the villagers came to watch this madman swinging on the platform, buffeted about by high winds. He took one month to complete the work and lost twenty-five pounds before it was finished. He succeeded in making an impression of the inscriptions, including texts hitherto unread, and he solved the mystery of how the artisans had reached that place to carve the monument. A pathway had been made up the mountain, and the upper forty feet of it is still there. The lower sixty feet had been laboriously chipped away so that it was unusable. Darius had made certain that the carving would not be destroyed.

David Stronach, Director of the British Institute for Persian Studies in Iran, himself a world-famous archeologist, went with Cameron some years later with ropes and ladders and they climbed up again. David laughingly told me he was so nauseated by the height that he couldn't read the inscription, but he did determine they had been originally worked with a "toothed chisel" to scarify the stone.

I was lucky enough to meet Cameron, who had returned to Iran while we were there. When I attended a meeting of the International Symposium of Archeologists, his fellow archeologists suggested we give a dinner to honor our distinguished countryman for his work at Bisitun and his deciphering of many of the "treasury" tablets found at Persepolis. We did give a dinner, but I put a price on it. I asked George to spend two hours in the museum with me reading and explaining the tablets.

His excitement and enthusiasm were contagious. One of the sections he had read at Bisitun from a badly damaged portion of the Old Persian inscription was a passage in which Darius said, "This is what I did in the second and third year of my reign." Then he went on to discuss two things: the suppression of a rebellion in Susiana and his conquest of some Scythians who "lived beyond a river."

George said that a few years ago he and one of his former students proved, in separate articles, that this latter conquest was none other than the famous attack on the Scythians who lived around the Sea of Azov in southern Russia, an attack which is described in detail by the Greek historian Herodotus. They also proved that the "river" crossed was none other than the Hellespont and the Dardanelles. The carvings were not rough, but as George told me, "almost exquisitely executed." Scholars, he said, now believe that by the end of the third full year of Darius's reign, 518 B.C., the scribes, stone cutters, and sculptors had finished their work.

Now, twenty-five hundred years later, it is still there for all to see. We pulled and scratched our way over jagged boulders and large rocks as far up as we could possibly get, but it was impossible to come within one hundred feet of the monument, which was almost directly overhead and carved into a slight recess. It appeared dwarfed by the mountain, but its breadth was over fifty feet and its height twenty-three feet, and one sizable chunk, where part of the inscription is carved, threatens to fall off.

After Darius's death in 486 B.C., the Greeks defeated his son, Xerxes I, on both land and sea, and Darius II, probably Darius's grandson, lost Egypt. The golden age of Persia was over, and after a succession of losses and fighting amongst its leaders, Persia was conquered and occupied in 330 B.C. by Alexander the Great. Across the territories of the Achaemenians from Macedonia to Taxila, in present-day Pakistan, Alexander marched his extraordinary army. He conquered Babylon and stayed there for some weeks before marching on to Susa, four hundred miles to the southeast. Susa had already surrendered to Philxenos, one of Alexander's generals. The Greeks left it intact but took its fabulous wealth, spoils of victory in earlier battles. Some of the gold was sent to finance Alexander's campaign in Sparta, and some of the priceless artifacts went back to Greece.

In his anxiety to be recognized by the Persians as their leader, Alexander even tried seating himself in Darius's throne, under its gold canopy. Perhaps he did not know, or perhaps he chose to defy, the legend that this would mean death to anyone other than the rightful occupant.

Some weeks later Alexander marched to Persepolis, four hundred miles further east, with hundreds of guides and men. Darius III had fled to the north where he was later captured and killed by traitors, and his body turned over to Alexander. For the Achaemenians, Persepolis had been the site of New Year festivities, which are still celebrated at Now Ruz to this day. In that period emissaries from every corner of the empire came at the New Year to pay homage and bring gifts to the king of kings. Scenes of this ritual are depicted on the remaining east staircase of the apadana. Nineteen different nationalities, from the Ethiopians to the Indians, are pictured carrying gifts and leading animals in the sculptured relief that climbs the staircase.

Alexander did not leave Persepolis until the late spring. Was he waiting for the Persian New Year, celebrated in March, the procession and the ritual of renewing allegiance to the recognized king? That year the emissaries never came. Nevertheless, Alexander held a great feast and Persepolis was burned, either by accident or design. Iranian scholars believe that Alexander allowed Persepolis to be destroyed, or at least all but the palaces and the citadel where the treasure was stored. (Even today Iranians bitterly resent the destruction of Persepolis, which Alexander justified by citing Persian crimes against the Greeks.) Fortunately for the historians, the heat of the fire had hard-baked hundreds of clay tablets and the glaze on the apadana relief and other remains uncovered later. They probably would not have survived if it had not been for the fire.

In that same year, two centuries after Cyrus's death, the Greek historians recorded that Alexander visited Cyrus's tomb at Pasargadae, perhaps to pay his respects to another great general. Before leaving Persepolis on his long march north and east across the Hindu Kush to Afghanistan, Baluchistan, and the Indus Valley to conquer the Achaemenian territories, he ordered the tomb to be well cared for. When he returned to Pasargadae in 325 B.C. and discovered the tomb had been vandalized, he was furious. Not even under torture did the guards reveal who had taken the gold sarcophagus, the royal robes, the jewelry, and the other treasures.

The tomb is one of the most moving sights in Persia. It stands alone, dominating what must have been a fertile plain, now bare except for the remains of other monuments. The steps up to it are about four feet wide. The gabled tomb chamber rises from the six stepped tiers, with only one narrow doorway. If you stand today on the Dasht-e Morghab, the plain of Pasargadae, Alexander's presence is eerily real. You may not know where he crossed the plain, but you do know that he stood on those steps, by the narrow door on the northwest facade, to pay homage to the man who conquered Astyges the Mede, and then constructed a palace as a memorial to that victory.

Absolute power had not brought Alexander peace, but rather great physical stress and delusions of grandeur. On his return to Susa he declared himself a god, and to further his dream of a new world state he ordered the famous mass marriage between Greeks and Iranians to celebrate the greatest expedition in recorded history.

His death in Babylon on June 13, 323 B.C. is still a mystery. Debilitated by too much wine (drunk in those days because the water was bad and unsafe), did he die of malarial fever? Or, as circumstantial evidence suggests, was he poisoned, perhaps by his old tutor Aristotle?

An aerial view of the late Shah's winter palace on the island of Kish in the Persian Gulf.

About twenty-three hundred years later Vice President Nelson Rock-efeller visited Iran. The Shah received him at his winter palace on the ancient island of Kish, which had been visited by one of Alexander's admirals: Nearchus. Three times in his informal speeches, presumably believing he was being wholly complimentary (or only aware of the romanticized version of Alexander), the Vice President likened the Shah to Alexander. To the Shah, Alexander represented a rapacious invader who destroyed Persepolis and stole Persian wealth. I watched the Shah's face as his eyes opened wide at the words of his old and good friend.

After Alexander's death there followed years of savage and bloody struggle for power between his surviving army commanders, and even-tually the direct line from Alexander became extinct. The Seleucis dy-nasty emerged and then the Parthians, a nomadic tribe, moved in from northeast Iran. They defeated the aggressive Romans in two important battles and prevented their expansion onto the plateau, and successfully defended their lands against the Scythian hordes from the north.

Again, in 211 A.D., descendants of the Achaemenians revolted and Ardeshir became the first of thirty Sasanian rulers. Taking their name from *sasan,* or commanders, they fostered a city-centered culture. Un-fortunately, the archeologists know very little about the form or the exact borders of their empire, their capital at Ctesiphon, near modern-day Baghdad, and the Shahanshah, their leader who not only ruled Iranshah (which included Iraq and what was then Bahrain), but also parts of Georgia, Armenia, Afghanistan, and southern central Asia.

In the Sasanian period, Jondi-Shapur in Khuzestan became a center of learning, particularly famous for medicine. Scribes became important in a country where priests, warriors, peasants, and artisans had held sway.

Because of the rise in use of the scribes, there are many seals surviving from that time. Some were used on documents, some worn as rings, some cylindrical; all are a great source of historical information.

The Sasanian Empire, exhausted by the struggle with Byzantine ag-gressors, fell to the Islamic nation. Mohammad, a simple man of Mecca, had changed the entire course of Iranian history.

8

Dinners, Visitors, and a Ming Jar

The guest is the donkey of his host.

On August 8, 1974, Dick and I telephoned a friend in Washington. He told us that President Nixon would be talking on television that evening, and there was speculation he would announce his resignation, thus bringing the Watergate scandal to a climax. The speech was at 9 P.M., Washington time—4:30 A.M. our time. I wanted to get up, feeling it was a historical moment I did not want to miss, but Dick was convinced it would be just another placating justification of the President's conduct; he said he had no intention of losing sleep listening to it.

A U.S. marine always spent the night in a small room on the ground floor of the residence. I asked him to awaken me at 4:15 A.M. When he called I got up, rather regretting my decision, and put on my dressing gown. I picked up my large shortwave radio and went down to sit in the garden. The reception was always much clearer outside the building. We could seldom get the Voice of America because the signal was too weak for satisfactory reception in Iran, but eventually I found the speech carried live on a Swedish station.

It was a warm, starry night, and the lovely garden looked like a fairyland, brightened by the security lights. I was sure all the Iranian guards standing on duty around the house and under the trees were watching me, and they must have been curious when one of the bedroom windows flew up noisily and Dick, unable to stand the suspense any longer, called to me, asking for news. The guards probably thought there was some fiery domestic quarrel taking place between the ambassador and his wife.

For us it was a dramatic and sobering moment. We were filled with a sense of history, and, I must confess, relief. We had found that although the diplomats we knew attempted to show sympathy for the plight of the President of the American people, few foreigners understood the entire Watergate episode. From what Dick told me, the Shah liked the President, and he admired his grasp of geopolitics and world affairs. (Nixon apparently thought equally well of the Shah, since he was one of the few to attend the Shah's funeral in Cairo in July 1980.) The Shah was not happy to see President Nixon go, but it was clear that he was disturbed at the paralysis that was afflicting American foreign policy. Now a new page had turned at last and we would face the future with President Ford, who had none of the same baggage to carry.

During the previous tumultuous months Dick had returned to Washington several times to testify before Congress on the Watergate break-ins, and at those times I had stopped going to official functions. When an ambassador leaves his post the second in command at the embassy becomes the chargé d'affaires. At this time the ambassador's wife virtually becomes nonexistent, because her role is only in support of her husband.

But another ambassador told me I was wrong to stop attending the Iranians' functions. He pointed out to me that Persians are poets, not diplomats. "They don't understand these pure legalisms of your State Department," he said. "They had a civilization long before us and they appreciate what you represent." He added that Iran was not like Europe; it was an offense to the Iranians if you did not go to their functions.

One evening when Dick was away I went, somewhat tentatively, to a reception at the Foreign Ministry, where the senior minister present greeted me at once. He thanked me very charmingly for coming and said that because of my earlier absences they had thought I did not like them and was not happy in Iran. I assured him that I was happy in Iran, and explained that I had only stayed away while Dick was out of the country. Now Dick's trips to the States were over, for the moment at least.

We were hoping that Henry Kissinger, who had succeeded William Rogers, would remain as Secretary of State to provide continuity in foreign policy. We wondered how strong a President Mr. Ford would be. Nevertheless, our working days went on as before. We got up early every morning, partly because every day was tightly scheduled and there were always unexpected events besides. If we had wanted to sleep late, it would have been impossible anyway; the policemen below our window began laughing and chattering at dawn. Even during the night we were lucky if they kept their voices down.

Farooq knocked on our door at 7 A.M. and we went downstairs for breakfast in the small family dining room. This gave us a chance to read the *Times* of London and the *International Herald Tribune,* both of which always arrived one day late. At breakfast Dick also received a wrap-up of the latest world news, prepared locally by the staff of the United States Information Agency. At eight o'clock he walked across the compound to the office, in time for the early morning staff meeting. Iranians also went to work early as many offices closed during the afternoons.

At eight-thirty I started my Persian lesson, but it was interrupted numerous times by telephone calls. Our social obligations were handled by the social secretary, whose office was in the chancery. The calls that came directly to me were from visitors in town, or from my friends and acquaintances.

One morning a week I played cards with my Iranian women friends. They had been kind enough to ask me to join them, and these were happy occasions as Iranians are fierce card players. The conversation was light and gossipy; there was never any discussion of internal politics. If the royal family was mentioned, it was only in the context of enlisting their influence. But I was always home by lunchtime. Most husbands were home in time for a late lunch, and ladies' luncheons were not a custom in either the diplomatic corps or among the Iranians themselves. Dick and I took this time to get to know members of the embassy staff or to invite an Iranian in to tell us about some particular area of interest to us. It was one of the ways to learn; at diplomatic dinner parties there is seldom any substantive conversation.

Dick usually left his office at five in the afternoon and we would play tennis, either singles or doubles with another couple from the embassy. We had a very active embassy tennis team, for which Dick and I played as a mixed doubles couple. The first year, when our team lost a match to the Iranian Foreign Ministry, there were headlines in the paper: "Foreign Ministry Trounces the American Embassy." I had a small bet with my husband, and sure enough, when we won the next year there was no mention of this in the newspaper. But we enjoyed the exercise tennis gave us. Certainly we needed it if we were to keep up with our heavy schedule.

Since I moved in different circles from my husband during the daytime, I would often tell him of particularly interesting people I had run into; in my enthusiastic way I would end by saying, "You might enjoy meeting them." If he agreed, we would ask the social secretary to invite them, and then often the trouble would start. An Iranian of very fixed ideas, the secretary was extremely efficient and knowledgeable about Iranian protocol and translating official invitations. Educated in England, she told me the first day we met, in a pronounced English accent, that she did not like women and preferred not to work with them. There were set guest lists that she had been using for years and we were anxious to augment them. She seldom approved of my suggestions, and she certainly did not approve when I succeeded in putting together a group of artists and people interested in the arts to come and see the collection of paintings that we brought with us to Iran.

On one occasion I wanted to invite a particular doctor I had met, and this lady told me he was not the sort of person that should be invited to the embassy. When he was made a cabinet minister a week later, I felt vindicated. But I was more concerned with making an effort to meet the ordinary citizen and not just the so-called elite. It was an uphill struggle, and I often resorted to other ways of inviting people. This was not easy, partly because of the communications problems. There was no local telephone book and, because of the tight security, the guards at the gate had to be informed when a guest was coming. Even so, there was no assurance of gaining admittance. If the guards were not able to read a written invitation, the guest was turned away at the gate, a rather discouraging rejection after a long hot ride.

It all took more strength, time, and tenacity to accomplish than it would have at home, but there *were* ways to do it, and I tried to take advantage of some of them. We gave a supper for the American Field

Service students who came each year for the summer, and we included the local families they were to live with during their stay. I was surprised at the effort and distance that some of the families traveled just to attend, and how excited they seemed to be invited to the American embassy.

When the director of the American Museum in Britain wrote to me to ask if we would receive a group he was bringing to Tehran, I thought they might enjoy something more than just a dinner party or reception. I worked with a collector to put on an unusual display of Qashqa'i lion rugs. In the process I realized that collectors feel about their rugs the way prima donnas feel about their singing roles. With a lot of help, we mounted the rugs on steel frames and displayed them around the garden; they looked magnificent, the lions marching across the garden with our compound trees and the distant mountains as a backdrop. Lions represent strength and courage and are not usually a pattern for traditional Iranian rugs; but these were woven in Fars Province, in the past a land of royal households. Supposedly, the women wove them as a tribute to their husbands, but some of the lions were so odd looking this might not always have been a compliment.

Lion rug woven by the Qashqa'i tribe of southwestern Iran. Inscribed and dated "Ordered by Nasrollah Khan in the year 1336" (1917 A.D.). Wool, 7'2 1/2" × 4'11"—*Collection of Parviz Tanavoli*

As we became more involved in Iranian society, we were able to see how differently it operated from our own and to understand how complex some of these differences are. For example, informal and sometimes secret groupings had political influence because of the absence of political institutions so familiar in the West. All over the country the daily meeting places for the people are the *qahvehkhanehs* and *chaykhanehs,* the coffee and tea houses. Often each one has its own group of patrons, sometimes divided by trade or guild membership. For instance, the cobblers may meet at a particular tea house. These houses represent an informal power base, sometimes political, sometimes not. There were more than two thousand of them in Tehran in the mid-seventies.

For the upper and middle classes, the *dowrehs,* which are a kind of men's club, are important and often have considerable influence. As we came to know more Iranians better, some unlikely friendships and alliances were explained by the fact that they belonged to the same *dowreh.* Most channels to power in Iran are informal, a tradition which goes back centuries in the belief that the lowliest citizen may petition the king or other high authority. A driver, servant, or secretary could be used by a petitioner to present his grievance or his request to the proper official.

In the Shah's case, any of the people around him were used as conduits: senators, military officers, personal friends, perhaps his stable boy, often his Court aides. Dick never had breakfast at the Court Minister's house without noting petitioners standing patiently at his gate. Other people close to the Shah had their own network of advisers, friends, and relatives. Constant jockeying and lots of ingenuity was used to gain a foothold in that power base. This ingenuity may take the form of *pul* (money), or even straight pushiness. An example of this power through proximity rather than normal occupational channels is the case of the son of the Shah's chauffeur, who made all the press announcements at the time of the Shah's exile in 1979.

Although Dick and the Shah attended the same school in Switzerland, they never met there, persistent press reports to the contrary. The first time they actually met was in 1957 when Dick was visiting Tehran. I had first met the Shah in 1968 when my son graduated from Harvard. I sat in Cambridge watching a small demonstration against the Shah, not feeling very involved and certainly not thinking that my life would ever be influenced by Iran or that I would ever see the Shah again.

After our arrival in 1973, Dick met with the Shah often. At their first audience Dick noticed that when he offered the Shah a cigarette, His

Majesty carefully took one of his own, even though Dick instantly accepted what was offered him. The King's fear of poison was almost second nature. The Shah later gave up smoking and on several occasions told Dick how much better he felt as a result. He was the first to notice when Dick, who had smoked for over forty years, suddenly stopped in Tehran. But Dick swore he really didn't feel any different.

Dick and the Shah always talked alone, and up to a point had free and frank conversations. Dick came home one afternoon after he had been to the palace and told me that while they had been talking, the phone rang beside the Shah's chair. This was unusual as he was never interrupted during an audience. When he put down the receiver, he told Dick that an Iraqi plane had been hijacked and that in spite of putting obstructions on the runway at the Tehran airport, the plane had landed off to one side. Dick remarked that he had not heard about the hijacking. The Shah replied, "I know you didn't know about it. It is just going on. I have given orders that the Iraqi ambassador is to be consulted and his approval sought to storm the plane." The conversation resumed on other issues. Again the phone rang and the Shah listened intently. He then said, "The event is over. The hijackers have surrendered. We did not need to assault the plane."

Under Iranian law hijacking is punishable by death. A senior Iranian police official was quoted the next day by a member of the embassy as saying, "The hijackers will receive a fair trial. They will then be shot."

On special holidays, or days of celebration like his birthday, the Shah held salaams in Golestan Palace. Dressed in full military uniform, with medals and gold braid, he received the diplomatic corps, government, local and other dignitaries. Sometimes, because of the number of people involved, this went on all day, with everybody fitted into the schedule. At the time of the New Year, the Empress received the wives of the diplomatic corps and presented each with a token momento of a small gold Pahlavi coin. On a previous Tuesday evening Dick and I learned of the delightful ceremony of *chahar shambeh suri.* It is an old Zoroastrian ceremony in which one jumps over the fire to get rid of the bad life of the old year and absorb the warmth of the New Year.

There were many heads of state who came to see the Shah. Not only did we meet these dignitaries at official receptions, but often Dick would see them privately if our government wished to communicate with them while they were in Iran. We met Madame Gandhi, the Prime Minister of India; Giscard d'Estaing, the President of France; King Khalid of

Saudi Arabia; President Anwar Sadat of Egypt; Sultan Qabus of Oman; President Senghor of Senegal; and the most colorful of all, Sheikh Rashid of Dubai. King Hussein, a personal friend of the Shah, came often to visit him privately (although he later declined to attend the Shah's funeral). During one of these visits Dick received a telegram from Washington instructing him to go to see King Hussein on a sensitive matter. Dick discovered that protocol demanded that he get permission from the Shah to visit another chief of state when he was a guest in the country. After obtaining the permission, Dick flew to the Caspian where King Hussein, whom he had known for a long time, was staying in one of the Shah's guest houses.

The Shah used two palaces in Tehran: Niavaran in the winter and Sa'dabad in the summer. A current of air came through one of the mountain passes, making the latter cooler during the hot months. Important guests of their Majesties usually stayed at the Sa'dabad guest house. Both the Kissingers on one of their visits and Mrs. Lyndon Johnson, the wife of the late President, stayed there, although she and her party did not find it very comfortable. It sounds very grand, but in those days it was badly in need of remodeling and air-conditioning.

Many of their Majesties' dinners were held at Niavaran Palace. Guests were summoned to arrive at a specific time. The security at the front gate was very tight, but our driver knew the drill and so we were never kept waiting. We would be met at the front door by the grand master of ceremonies and ushered into the main drawing room. These were very elegant evenings with their Majesties joining the guests for about half an hour before dinner was served. They would move around together, talking informally to everyone, and then would precede us into the state dining room.

The Shah always preceded the Empress into the room. Normally a shy, rather remote man, he was relaxed and friendly on these social occasions. Some found him a little humorless most of the time. The scar on his lip, caused in a 1949 attempt on his life, gave him a slightly cynical appearance. During the day he usually wore a double-breasted navy blue suit, and always stood ramrod straight. I could never decide whether this was because of his military training or to give him greater height. At state dinners the Shah and the Empress sat next to each other in chairs larger than those of the other guests on one side of a long or horseshoe-shaped table. At smaller dinners they sat opposite each other at the table.

Each place had its own hand-painted menu and place card beside the numerous pieces of vermeil cutlery. Every piece of glass and china was decorated with the royal emblem, which included the inscription in Persian, "He ordered me to be just and He is the one who will pass judgment." On one occasion I was surprised when the Shah pulled out my chair. This in itself was unusual, and with uncommon enthusiasm he said, "Mrs. Helms, I hear you have been translating our folk stories."

I told him that I was really enjoying them and my Persian studies. I added that I would not dare to speak to him in Persian as I might not use the correct tense. (My teacher had warned me and had given me a long list of greetings used for the royal family only.) He smiled, and we went on to discuss his country's poets. I mentioned that I was having a class at the embassy in poetry, and I told him the Dutch ambassador had persuaded me to go gliding, which interested him.

The Shah loved to fly and his half-sister, Princess Fatemeh, was both a helicopter and a fixed-wing pilot. Her son had just soloed at the age of eleven, and the Crown Prince shortly after gained his wings at the age of thirteen. No doubt because so many of the royal family were pilots, flying in Iran had been given special attention and the civilian flying clubs were well organized and the equipment was the best available. As for my experience, although the thermals and the planes were good, after a few flights over Tehran and coming in to land between the Iranian Air Force's Phantom jets, I decided it was not for me. I was scared.

As the caviar was served, I asked the Shah if it was true that he didn't like it. He had never been seen eating it. He told me he liked it very much but that he was allergic to all fish. As I listened to him, I thought if he had only become more personally popular with his people, Savak would not have cast such a shadow over the land.

It was not only difficult but almost impossible for me to find out what Savak was doing. I still believe that if it had been as all-pervasive and efficient as it was reported to have been, the revolution would not have been as successful or have come as such a surprise to the Shah. Dick often told me that he wondered if Savak told His Majesty the truth in their reporting or whether, like many other Iranians, they were just anxious to please him.

It was hard for me to ask questions as everybody was very nervous about discussing the organization. I did not know until later that a government minister had been ordered by the Shah to do a private study to determine whether there was any evidence of torture by Savak, only to be visited by Savak three days later. There is no doubt that Savak was tough, but Iran has a brutal heritage. The penitents whipping themselves with chains on the religious commemorations of Ashura is public witness to this. The statistics on political prisoners and the use of torture reported in the media have never been substantiated. I do not know the validity of these reports, but I do believe that in a few years, when there is less conjecture and more objective reporting, conclusive studies will turn up more accurate information on this period of Iranian history.

One young woman who called on me happened to tell me that her brother-in-law was in prison. He was arrested upon his return from Germany, where he had been active in an anti-Shah student organization. Members of his family were not told at the time why or when he had been arrested. They just knew that he had disappeared. Later they were allowed to visit him every week, and she said he was as comfortable as anybody could be when confined in a prison. He was allowed to pursue his studies and he taught classes for other prisoners every morning. They did not have any idea when he would be allowed out.

We had many different dinners to give and one of them was in honor of the dean of the diplomatic corps, the Russian ambassador. A date was set, both Mr. and Mrs. Erofeev accepted, and we invited what we thought would be a congenial group of diplomats and Iranians. There were to be thirty-six guests, the number that our dining room table could seat for a formal dinner. The secretary seated it very carefully according to protocol. I had brought with me from the United States tall gilt centerpieces with the flowers designed to hang gracefully down. They made ideal centerpieces since they did not block the view of the person opposite at the table. Set with the embassy's Lenox glassware and the off-white china with the gold band and U.S. crest on every piece, the table looked beautiful.

We awaited our guests in the drawing room, and as the dean walked through the front door, he announced that he was alone because "Madame is in Moscow." By this time Dick and I had already developed a system for just such emergencies. As it was a formal dinner, and the wife of the guest of honor was missing, the guests would have to be reseated. This necessitated the changing of many places, not just the few of lower rank. I alerted the wife of the deputy chief of mission that I was going to slip out so that she could take over as hostess while I was gone.

It takes a little time to reseat a dinner like that. Ministers must be in order of precedence as defined by their countries' protocol, and an ambassador's seniority derives from the length of time he has served in the host country. The wives assume the rank of their husbands for seating arrangements. I knew from personal experience how important this is. Living in Washington, I had seen officials, and even wives, very upset if they were not seated properly. There, more than once, ambassadors had refused to be seated until the arrangement had been changed. At a dinner for a Presidential candidate whom the hostess had seated on her right as the guest of honor, the French ambassador had demanded he take that seat, pointing out that the slight was not to him personally but to his country. This was not an isolated instance. I have witnessed it many times, even at small family suppers where a diplomat was included. This was not the only difficulty that could arise. I always kept a pen and place cards handy, as many times an unexpected guest, such as a wife who had been out of town, would suddenly return home in time for the dinner.

On the night of the dinner for the Soviet ambassador, Dick escorted the wife of the ranking minister of the Iranian government into dinner, and I asked the Russian ambassador to sit on my right. We had planned a simple but good dinner to be served by candlelight: soup, roast veal, salad and cheese, and crepes suzette flambé. This dessert was always a sensation. I don't know what Luigi, our Italian cook, used, but they continued to flame while the servants served all the guests. We had a large screen hiding the kitchen door and as the four waiters followed each other out holding high the flaming dishes, guests were inevitably awed by the spectacular sight. Nowhere else in the world have I seen this dessert served so dramatically.

After dinner we had no separation of the men and women. We served coffee and liqueurs in the large drawing room and, like all diplomatic dinners, it was over when the ranking guest, in this case the Russian ambassador, departed. At all formal dinners, diplomatic or private, when there is an official guest of honor, other guests allow him the courtesy of being the first to leave. Those guests who have an early morning start can sometimes be seen glaring at the guest of honor if he has not left by 11 P.M. If he does not want to leave because he is having such a good time, I have seen him go out of the door to release the other guests of their obligation, drive around the block, and come back in again.

As I discovered, there was a lot that could be learned about another culture at the dining table. You will see well-educated, widely traveled, sophisticated Iranians who have known each other for years sit side by side at a dinner and not speak to each other all evening. Not one word. I first noticed this because, as a hostess, I was concerned that I might have accidentally seated mortal enemies together. I finally asked an Iranian about it. She laughed and replied that this was an accepted custom. It is called being *qahr.* As she explained it to me, it seemed like a very sensible way of dealing with hostilities. *Qahr* is a word that is hard to translate, but it is much more than "not on speaking terms." It is more a way of breaking off communications, or agreeing to a cooling-off period, instead of exchanging heated and damaging words or threats which could only exacerbate a situation.

Most of the Iranian dinners in Tehran are buffets rather than formal affairs. Exceptions were those at the palace and at the Foreign Ministry. The Iranians seemed more comfortable with this informality, and it gave the men and the women a chance to congregate together. Custom and hospitality call for a laden and bountiful table, even if it ensures later sacrifice. Americans cook for the number of guests to be served. Iranians —at least the well-to-do—cook for the guests, the servants, and all the drivers of the guests, and often what is left over goes to the street sweepers. Bread is not only scarce, it is holy, and should not be thrown away. As the price of food was rising along with the income of the servants, this custom was beginning to change, but still there was always a generous gesture in both rich and poor households of "everything I have is yours." Occasionally one must have the wit not to accept this at face value. A family's food for a whole week may be on the table.

For our first Iranian buffet, we should have been well briefed. We were not and nearly starved. Today's buffet is a modification of an ancient tradition. In the past, the *sofreh,* or cloth, was spread on the ground and guests seated round it to eat the food from bowls within their reach. With no forks or knives, the meat was folded into unleavened bread. The modern version involves tables and chairs or cushions. Food is served late as you are expected to leave right after eating. Unlike an American buffet, where you get your food and move on around the table, you do not move in Iran. Nobody moves. You find a plate and then you become single minded about finding a few vacant inches near the table. You may be dressed to kill, wearing both your jewels and an evening gown, but somehow you have to use your pointed elbows to squeeze in between single-minded people locked in food and conversation. So it is imperative that your chosen site of approach be at least within piercing distance of the food.

Many Americans who came to Iran as official guests would show by the end of their stay their appreciation of a seated, served dinner. They had often given up all idea of sampling Persian food and had concentrated on the large bowls of caviar luxiously available at most tables. That was a far better approach for their short stay than that used by the people who insisted on avoiding local food entirely and ordering what they thought would be a recognizable American dish. This turned out to be true only on the menu. I traveled with an oil company executive whose American local manager's wife insisted upon ordering American food for him as we traveled. Fortunately, he had been there many times before and knew that local Iranian dishes are excellent.

Americans came in droves as the guests of the Iranian government. Some arrived on free plane trips, arranged by the Iranian ambassador in Washington, or came for film festivals, or to give their expert opinions on a number of development projects. The annual film festival brought us a wide variety of guests, but the plans for the festival tended to be ambitious in terms of the local facilities. The high-powered stars and directors invited were often bewildered by the lack of arrangements made for them. On the morning we were to give a large luncheon for the group, I received a telephone call from one of the stars asking if she might bring her baby because she was nursing it. I assured her this would be no problem as we had plenty of bedroom space she could use. To the consternation of my husband, who had been lulled into an unambassadorial mood by Candice Bergen asking him for his autograph, he found the mother nursing her baby in the front hall and no amount of persuasion would move her. Fortunately, for our peace of mind, we did not know that one guest who arrived very late had been in the bazaar. Forgetting that she was in a Moslem country, she was scantily dressed and seemed surprised that the glances and remarks thrown at her had not been all that admiring. She was lucky that she caused no untoward incident.

We loved to have our American friends to stay with us. Many of them came and we had many official guests as well. Never once did the servants complain. In fact, they seemed to enjoy the entertaining as much as we did. I came to look upon them as my official family and when we ourselves traveled throughout the Persian Gulf area to Saudi

Arabia, Bahrain, and the other sheikhdoms, we found that through some mysterious form of desert communication Pakistani friends of theirs would mysteriously appear and offer help and services, and sometimes give us a letter to take back.

Their way of life seemed harsh to us. They left their wives and children at home in Pakistan and returned to see them every two years, presumably with whatever money they had saved. They seemed to accept this passively but a week seldom passed when one of them did not have bad news from home. Wives and families seemed to suffer a series of disasters: Houses were washed away in floods, children died, fathers arrived home on a wet Tuesday with another wife, causing the first wife and mother untold misery and often deprivation.

I always knew when something was wrong. Their soft brown eyes would brim with emotion as I inquired if all was well at home. But one day I was very irritated when Farooq, as the spokesman, told me the manservant of a very senior U.S. military man who had been staying with us had borrowed money from the servants, ostensibly because he did not have any of the local currency. He had left without repaying them. I sat right down and wrote to the officer, asking him if he would be kind enough to see that the money was returned. He wrote back a very supercilious letter that said he was not responsible for this debt. I refunded all the money to Farooq myself and extracted a promise from him to lend nothing more, however appealing the request.

We were very fortunate to meet many of the scholars working in different fields in Iran. They added a dimension to our lives and our knowledge that we could not have acquired any other way, particularly as so much of their recent work would not get into print for many years. One particular day stands out in my memory because so many strange things fell into place within twenty-four hours. Early one morning I had a telephone call from an Iranian friend. We had talked about Chinese porcelain many times, and she told me she had just been offered a large porcelain bowl. It was being sold at a very reasonable price. Nevertheless, she wanted it authenticated before she bought it. I explained that my knowledge was very limited, but she wanted me to see it.

She picked me up and we drove to the house of a retired school teacher who apparently augmented his income by selling artifacts. He showed us many pieces and eventually produced the bowl that made everything else look second rate. It was an exquisite, large, blue and white bowl in perfect condition. I copied the marks on it very carefully, all the while remembering to look nonchalant so that he didn't increase the price. We went back to the residence, where I showed her some large shards that were almost identical in pattern. I had picked them up on the beach of the island of Hormoz and had sent them back to the Freer Gallery of Art, where they had enthusiastically identified them as belonging to the Ming period. They were obviously relics from the old porcelain trade routes through the Persian Gulf. My friend's bowl was identical and the marks confirmed this. I wanted to be very cautious about recommending that she buy it, so I telephoned the British Institute for Persian Studies and asked David Stronach if they had an expert on Chinese porcelain on their staff. He said no, but within a few hours he called back.

"Cynthia," he said, "the most extraordinary coincidence has just happened. A Chinese porcelain expert from the British Museum has just walked through the door of my office."

I raced up to his office in the north of town to get Stronach's visiting expert, and together we went to look at the bowl. She was very excited about it and confirmed my suspicions. In appreciation for her help, I asked her to join my husband and me for dinner. We had planned a rare quiet evening. As we walked through to the dining room, we passed a large commonplace jar that I had bought the day before. I had found it on the floor of a junk shop and had no idea what it represented, but I knew the moment I saw it that it looked and felt special. So for a few dollars I bought it and carried it home. The porcelain expert took one look at it and turned in my direction.

"I suppose you know that is Ming," she said.

It had been a day collectors dream of.

9

Skeletons
at Hasanlu

A shroud does not have any pockets.

I soon decided that that which I could do best as the ambassador's wife and still be helpful to Dick was in areas not directly related to government business. An ambassador needs to stay informed about his host country, and what I could do—and what I delighted in doing because I wanted to learn—was expand our awareness of Iranian culture.

Dick encouraged me to travel throughout the country—to meet Iranians, to visit the many foreigners working in the field, to sightsee. Communication in Iran was extremely primitive and reports of events happening outside Tehran were frequently unreliable. Often the only way we could be sure of news from Iran's many remote provinces was to take a trip ourselves.

In late summer of 1975 a team of prehistorians returning from the field came to lunch at the embassy. Led by Professor Bernard Campbell of the University of California at Los Angeles, they had been searching for skeletons of an early stage in man's evolution, homonoid Ramapi-thicus, in the fossil bed on the eastern shore of Lake Reza'iyeh in the northwest province of Azarbayjan. They had found skeletons of early animals but not Ramapithicus. To make matters worse, they had suffered from terrible dysentery. One team member had lost forty pounds.

Dick and I sensed they were depressed about a return to the same site with a repetition of the same problems, and we asked if there was anything we could do to help. They seemed pleased that we were interested and invited us to visit their site. Dr. Hind Kooros, head of the Iranian Natural History Museum, and I planned to go together, since the museum was supplying some support facilities for the trip and was to receive specimens from the excavations. Dr. Kooros was an archeozoologist who had found evidence of homo Erectus in Azarbayjan Province in the 1960s; in the same decade she had also found a hand axe about two million years old.

We flew to Tabriz, a city with a strong Russian flavor, now the second largest city in Iran. Surrounded by mountains, in the old days it was a natural site for a caravanserai (a resting place used by early travelers), and it is still a major stopover on the main route for auto travel from Europe to the Far East. A sprawling, unattractive place, its bazaar is a hunting ground for Russian samovars, old Russian silver, and even some porcelain. Tabriz is also a center for modern craftsmen; its silversmiths and its carpets are famous.

Our flight was late. Hotels in Iran tended to be overcrowded and you could never be sure of your reservation, and this proved to be the case on our arrival. The hotel desk had given away our room. By the time we realized we weren't going to find another, it was 11 P.M. I knew the American consul and his wife were leaving for the United States the next day and were all packed up and ready to go, so we couldn't stay at their place. In desperation Hind called the head of the Iranian environmental office, who graciously invited us to stay at his home.

Hospitality in Iran is such that you can never go into a house without being fed. There is no such thing as potluck, and even at that hour we had to wait while a considerable meal was prepared. I looked at it with alarm and admiration—we had already eaten, and we were exhausted after our long day. How had our host's wife put all this together on such short notice? We heard a lot of whispering from behind closed doors. Had all the neighbors been pressed into service to supply the food?

We managed to eat, but I felt nervous about where we were going to sleep. Surreptitiously I poked around. There weren't any beds or any signs of a bedroom, just endless Persian carpets lying wall to wall in every room. In fact, there was no furniture in the house at all except a small telephone table.

At last our host appeared in the main reception room with two bedrolls and laid them carefully on the floor. We steeled ourselves for the Eastern style bathroom, where we attired ourselves appropriately, and then climbed into the bedding. I felt at a distinct disadvantage lying on a stranger's floor while the host kept hovering over us, asking if we had everything we needed. Worse still, I couldn't seem to stop my fits of nervous laughter, which covered my chagrin at having our hostess's only bedrolls when she was very pregnant. Eventually we fell asleep and we left early in the morning to drive south toward Miyaneh.

For some time Hind had been wanting to look for evidence of neolithic man in the caves in this area, and as we got out into the countryside she began to take our Land Rover off on one dirt road after another. She was looking for some caves she had spotted on a previous trip. We left our escorts—two men from the environmental office—drinking tea in the *chaykhaneh,* or tea house, and hiked around a small village until Hind found a promising cave entrance. We had borrowed a lamp from a small boy, but I felt uneasy because it flickered miserably; its light was not much bigger than a candle's flame.

Hind was a determined woman. As the cave opened up before us, she led the way deeper and deeper into the earth. Also, I pointed out, farther and farther from the cave's entrance, especially if our tiny lamp went out. But she was carried away. By now we were on our backsides, crawling through mud, holding up the light, looking for paintings on the walls. Suddenly I sensed a large emptiness right beside me. I put my hand down into nothingness. We were on the edge of a precipice. Even Hind thought we had gone far enough.

We arrived at Miyaneh tired, hot, dirty, and anxious to find our hotel room. Miyaneh is a fairly large town on the main route to Tabriz and it, like Tabriz, endured attacks by the Mongols. Our room was cleaner than most, but as usual had only one light bulb hanging in the middle, which made reading or relaxing difficult. We ate the national dish of *chelow kabab*—rice with ground lamb pounded into an elongated piece of meat with a raw egg broken over the rice. In Iran even the small remote places have appetizing food, and there is always good tea and fresh bread.

We decided to take the direct but unmapped road to Maragheh. We bought melons and something to drink, and persuaded our two companions that we were hardy and that they need not worry about our comfort. The dirt road wound through small villages, which became increasingly farther apart. Gradually we realized there was nothing in front of us except tracks, going in numerous directions, and we were suddenly astonished to see enormous road-building machines bulldozing what looked like four-lane highways miles from anywhere. With nothing, not even vegetation, visible for miles, they seemed especially incongruous. We never did discover why they were there.

Occasionally we saw a few distant trees and sometimes a lake; the latter always proved to be a mirage. We drove toward the trees, where we would find a tiny hamlet nestled around a stream or spring. This way we charted our route from hamlet to hamlet. Often the shepherds we asked did not know the name of the next settlement. (I remembered hearing a Prime Minister say Iran had sixty thousand villages, and when someone asked him how he knew, he smiled and said, "I don't—but you Americans always want statistics.") Sometimes we had to turn back and try another track, and our companions were visibly nervous that we were not going to find Maragheh by nightfall. But we did—just.

Maragheh is the site of one of the best-known fossil fields in the world. Over a hundred years ago a Russian traveling cross country on horseback noticed bones protruding from the hills south of Maragheh. He returned the following year, set up camp, and paid the local inhabitants to dig some specimens for him. These specimens he sold to museums. The fossils, seven to ten million years old, are found in a formation whose strata are visible for miles and miles, and because of the lack of vegetation it was easy to see the levels where the strata began and ended. The site was large and not until recently had it been scientifically excavated.

We found the team of prehistorians camping around a small unused schoolhouse in the village of Chellivand with their sleeping tents in a nearby orchard. They were led by Dr. John Vancouverin, a geologist who had spent many years in eastern Africa with an old friend of mine, Dr. Louis Leakey. Their health was better (the dysentery had been caused by a sewage pipe being crossed with a fresh-water pipe) and they had found a skeleton of a Hipparion horse—a short-necked giraffe which had huge antlers covered with skin—as well as many other animals. But still no Ramapithicus.

We added our food to their limited supply and set up our sleeping bags near theirs. After supper we listened to their plans for the next day's dig. At dark there was no electricity or anything to read by, so we went to bed. The next morning we were up at four-thirty. I took my cup of coffee and sat back in a corner, watching an atmosphere totally different from that of the night before. The scientists had fixed up a small lab in the schoolhouse, where one or two people always stayed behind to work on preserving the things they had found, and every day two of the group stayed to cook and clean up. The rest went to various areas of the site to photograph, survey, or continue excavation. The actual digging, of course, was done with enormous care; intricate methods were needed to excavate the fossils.

The end of the work outside came late in the morning as it got too hot under the sun's rays. Then everybody would work for the rest of the daylight hours in the lab indoors. After the long workday was finished, I sat with Dr. Vancouverin on the banks of a stream, while he explained to me his theory of how this large area must have looked as a savannah all those years ago. He told me that the animals probably died in a catastrophic drought and had been covered by pumice sediment from the nearby Sahand volcano deposited in the form of gigantic floods.

The villagers brought tea as we picnicked in their orchard at the end of the day. Outwardly, they appeared to lead an idyllic life. Theirs was a small hamlet in absolutely beautiful countryside surrounding a stream. There was ample fruit and nuts on the trees. The shepherds could be seen bringing home their flocks. But the chickens clucking around in the dark, dusty passageways—they hardly qualified as streets —looked extremely scrawny and the flies around the village were overwhelming.

When I looked at the children I wondered why they all had runny noses in the middle of summer and sores all over their bodies. I found out when I walked along the stream. While the women were washing the cooking utensils, their animals and their children with their dirty underwear or dirty behinds were there, too.

The villagers near one of the excavation sites were friendly, but the ones near the camp in the schoolhouse had a surly air. Members of the team took precautions not to walk around alone. The people were upset about erecting tents and parking Land Rovers in front of the schoolhouse. The reason for this turned out to be that they used this area for the storage and thrashing of shocks of grain. One expedition member had been an army medic and treated minor ailments and other problems of the villagers, which began to help relations.

It was interesting to see the first traces of modern agriculture starting to appear in a society which was still farming, irrigating, and harvesting with centuries-old techniques. Anachronisms were everywhere—there were new Mercedes buses competing with hay-laden donkeys for the right-of-way and tractors pulling stone-age thrashing devices. The people of Maragheh, a larger town, obviously disapproved of women in Western dress, sometimes vehemently.

As we left Maragheh we stopped at a farm for lunch with the cousin of a friend of mine, and had a lively discussion on the local agricultural problems. In 1962 Maragheh had become the first town to undergo land reform. Its agricultural lands are among the most fertile in the country. Our friends were discussing what had happened in this conservative area that had otherwise resisted modernization. Under the land reform plan, private and public unused land was distributed to the villagers over a number of years and through various programs. Reza Shah had introduced land-holding registration for tax purposes and when the landowners' villages and farms were distributed; the government used this base to calculate their remuneration. This policy could be known as an underestimation for an underestimation.

When the farmland was owned by a landlord, he kept his villagers as part of his family. He lived in the village and shared what he had. Half the country's cultivatable land was owned by the great landowners —not feudal ownership owing fealty to the Shah, but outright ownership as private property. Some landowners owned as many as sixty villages.

As modernization reached Iran, the landlords started migrating or traveling abroad and appointing others to collect their share of the crops from the villagers. Villagers were exploited, but the land reform was not so much a cry from the fields as a command from the throne. Reza Shah had laid the foundation, ideally to free the villagers from bondage, and his son continued the work. From 1951 to 1971 land reform became a national movement, with various programs to bring it about.

Distribution and reimbursement varied throughout the country, and there were problems. Without direction the villagers did not know when to plant crops and when to water, and there was no longer any central organization for cleaning, repairing, and maintaining the *qanats*

—the irrigation system—or allotting the water. It was hard to get credit to buy seed and fertilizer or to get much-needed irrigation pumps from the government. The merchants had extended credit during the winter months for necessities like salt and sugar, but often at exorbitant interest rates (in spite of the religious laws). Now they collected at harvest time and the villagers had to borrow again for the next planting. The Bank Omran had been formed for agricultural lending, but it had limited funds, and in the beginning could only service the areas resettled from the Pahlavi lands. Often nomads had been settled on these lands, particularly around the Caspian Sea, and it takes many years to make enlightened farmers out of nomads.

Listening to the distressing discussion, I recalled the talk I had heard as a child, living on a farm in England. There we had a constant reevaluation of methods and crops, complicated by the perennial adverse weather conditions. I had learned that farming is a difficult business, and not for inexperienced tillers of the land. The Iranian villagers needed not only the sort of help a well-organized extension service could give them, but marketing advice as well. And all this would be made more arduous by having to educate them to use these services. They were unable to surmount these difficulties, and more and more people were leaving and trying to find work in the cities.

As we drove on toward Hasanlu, we saw large pieces of farm machinery sitting unused in the fields. A Peace Corps volunteer told me these machines came from many countries with no spare parts and no servicing facilities, and when they broke down they were abandoned. The waste and unsophisticated buying of sophisticated machinery was evident throughout Iran. I remembered hearing about a plant in Shiraz. The people there needed pasteurized milk, but instead of taking the advice to buy machinery from one foreign source, they bought parts from many countries and the plant took six years to build.

In Hasanlu, Professor Robert Dyson of the University of Pennsylvania had been directing the archeological digs there every other season since 1957. I decided to go and see him, too, and find out if there was anything his team needed. But visiting an archeological or any field site entails a rather special protocol. Instead of a house present, you bring newspapers, magazines, and mail from the outside world. And you must not eat too much from any of their cherished rations. I was therefore greeted a little warily, since the wife of an ambassador is expected to be used to extravagant treatment. I knew Bob Dyson, but not the rest of the team. He had told me in Tehran that in his twenty years of excavating in Iran, that year was the first time he had been invited to the U.S. embassy for a dinner for international archeologists.

Hasanlu, an early Iron Age citadel, was a very exciting site for a nonprofessional to visit. The approach was pastoral; the attractive villages on the way were surrounded by orchards and vineyards. Some test excavations were started earlier, before Dyson had begun his excavations, but the long-term American project at Hasanlu had been very rewarding. For an amateur it was especially fascinating when Dyson, a quiet, gentle man, greatly admired by his peers, showed me around, enthusiastically explaining and recreating the ancient scene. Concentrating on the period just prior to the arrival of the Medes and the Persians in the first millennium B.C., the archeologists now had a well-defined citadel with ample evidence of streets and major public buildings and two- or three-story houses of sun-dried mud brick, set in mud mortar with framed doorways.

Situated at the western approach to a still unidentified kingdom south of Lake Reza'iyeh, there is evidence that the citadel was often attacked by Assyrians, Urartians, and the armies of other peoples. When the archeologists found more than forty skeletons uncovered inside one of the columned halls, it seemed to be a sad human story. The skeletons were all looking as if they were moving toward a doorway and many had been hit on the back of the head. The date of this apparent attack, probably by Urartians, is about 800 B.C. A young man and woman, their skeletons still embracing as if for protection, were found in a storage bin —probably suffocated when they crawled into the bin to escape the fire. A man's hand and arm were found clutching an exquisite solid gold bowl covered with repoussé representations of gods and goddesses riding chariots, animals, and birds. Other beautiful objects and attractive burnished gray pottery from the same time are now in the Tehran Archaeological Museum.

At this site I was allotted a small tent with a floor to reduce the danger of scorpions. I had a sleeping bag and my ski underwear because the nights were very cold. The others all slept in huts, but the team had obviously discussed that a stately tent was the way they should handle an ambassador's wife. We all used the primitive icy-cold outside washing bowl in rotation and went to bed early, me feeling silly with the two guards the Iranian government had insisted on giving me sitting stiffly outside my tent. (It was lucky Dick hadn't been able to come. To say he doesn't like camping is an understatement. The very thought of it sends shivers down his spine.)

The second night I gave up. What sounded like a hurricane-force wind was swinging and swaying the tent with a terrible roar. I felt as if the whole tent was going to be airborne. I had visions of the guards telling my husband I was last seen still in my tent, heading into the wind on a west-southwesterly course at a speed of approximately fifty miles an hour. I leapt through the door past the two sleeping guards and crept quietly to what I hoped were the women's quarters, once again an old schoolhouse. Guided by a wakeful young woman, I found an empty cot and curled up until I had to wake the guards at 5 A.M. for the camp face wash.

We left Hasanlu to drive north to meet Dick at Reza'iyeh. The route took us due west around the southern edge of Lake Reza'iyeh; we were in Kurdish country. The Kurds are located along the western border of Iran, as far south as the land of the Lurs, another nomadic tribe. The name Kurdistan is now given to that area, although it is not a separate province. This was Azarbayjan Province, and as Dick had been briefed so many times on what was going on there, he was anxious to visit the area.

Following World War II the Soviet Union established an autonomous state in Azarbayjan. In addition, a Russian-backed puppet government of Kurds set up the Republic of Mahabad in nearby Kurdistan. To Iranians it looked as though Russia would effectively detach these areas from Tehran's control and force Iran to grant Moscow major oil concessions. Thanks, however, to the United Nations and a determined President Harry S Truman, the Russians withdrew their troops in 1946, the Iranian Army moved into the region, and the puppet regimes collapsed, leaving the Shah once more in control of the northwestern segment of his country.

The Kurds, however, continued to be restless, egged on by their brethren in Iraq, who ran a constant campaign for autonomy at the least, or for an independent Kurdistan at the most. Turkey kept her Kurds under strict control and Iran watched hers carefully; but the Kurds in the mountain regions of Iraq, led by Mullah Mustafha Barzani, fought a constant military campaign against the Baghdad government. With the outbreak of the Arab-Israeli War in 1973, it became important for Iraqi troops to be pinned down as much as possible, so that Iraq could not bring additional manpower and equipment to bear on the Arab side

A Kurdish woman making yoghurt in northwestern Iran. (Lynn Salmi)

against the Israelis. Western support was provided secretly to the Barzani forces, not the least of which were arms and support equipment provided by the Iranians.

Iraq, disenchanted with the idea of a separate Kurdistan, resettled many of its Kurdish population, replacing them with Arabs, particularly in the area of the Karkuk oil fields. She also agreed to a border between the two countries at the Thalweg, the deepest part in the Shatt al-Arab River, if the Shah would cease supporting the Kurdish rebels. By the seventies, however, the Shah was very considerate of the Iranian Kurds. He supported them militarily and gave them good positions in the army and other areas of government. The Kurds, who are Sunnis, want an independent Kurdistan, which would include Kurds from southeast Turkey, northern Iraq (where twenty percent of the population is Kurdish), northwest Iran, and southwest Russia.

Driving back through the villages toward Tabriz, we saw that all the women on the streets were wearing the chador—it is a very conservative area. The governor's wife told me that, although she was an Iranian, she had been accosted when she appeared in Western dress. She was also having a problem communicating because many in Tabriz speak Turkish and she spoke only Persian. This brought home to us how difficult it is for any Iranian ruler to coordinate a cohesive central government.

We had a problem bartering in the village of Osku, known for its silk industry, because almost all of northwest Iran is Turkish-speaking, and even our drivers couldn't talk to the merchants. (The Turkish spoken is Azeri Turki. It differs from modern Turkish spoken in Turkey.) Dick gestured around his neck to mean "tie," and finally an old gnarled woman dug around in the baskets and produced ties we could buy. Iranians don't wear ties. The word *keravati* means a wearer of ties and denotes a Westernized person; this is one of the reasons you don't see members of Iran's new Islamic government wearing them.

We continued driving east to Astara along the Russian-Iranian border, which is twelve hundred miles long. In northeast Azarbayjan, the natural border is a deep chasm. This area is very different from the rest of Iran's arid areas and salt deserts. It is hard here, with the rich grassy valleys and densely wooded mountains, to remember the poor agricultural lands or food shortages. The land takes vast downward sweeps through broad wheat fields and lush pastures, all tilled at the most unlikely angle. All along the way to the left is the Russian frontier, unbroken forest with no sign of cultivation, just the eerie frontier guards in their lookout posts (small wooden huts on stilts) watching you watching them. The traffic is sparse and the ride is an eerie one.

There are now forty-four million Moslems in Russia and as they have a higher birthrate than other Russian peoples, it has been predicted that by the year two thousand out of a projected population of three hundred and eight million almost seventy-seven million would be of Moslem birth.

Astara is a large, seemingly relaxed town with red-roofed buildings, the terminus of the natural gas lines from southern Iran to Russia. As you drive around the Caspian Sea, the Alborz Mountains, so bare on their southern slope, dip down on this northern face to a subtropical forest area of swamps and terraced sea plantations, with rice paddies, a closed world of sea, and a great green wall of mountains. The sea is some eighty-five feet below sea level. It is far less saline than other enclosed water surfaces in the Middle East, such as the Dead Sea and Lake Reza'iyeh, and it is slowly shrinking about eight inches a year. Here we saw no more irrigation channels, few relics of ancient civilizations, and no donkeys or camels. Instead, we were impressed by the rich cultivation and crowded villages. In the summer the heat is thick and steamy.

Close to the sea the air is heavy and the vegetation lighter, although still relentlessly lush. The houses in from the shore are no longer domed and mud-walled, but are wooden-roofed with high-pitched thatch or shingles and are often on stilts because of the possibility of flooding. Even the mosques look different here. The peasants, who wear bright clothes, look wrinkled from generations of malaria and damp heat. Like Londoners, they carry umbrellas even on fine days. But they remind you more of Chinese coolies than Londoners, as they walk with large poles across their backs balancing heavy melon baskets.

We saw ungainly water buffalo in the swamps and splendid Turkoman horses in the fields. The Talesh hills below Rasht have a heavy rainfall and no really dry season. Besides rice, grown mainly on the marshy lowlands at or near sea level, sugar, cotton, tobacco, maize, tea, and citrus fruit grow in small fields on the higher ground. Extensive mulberry bushes support the silkworms.

Evidence has been found that paleolithic man lived here, and parts of the high areas of these hills still remain unknown and unpenetrated; the Caspian miniature horse depicted at Persepolis has been recently redis-covered here. Years ago there were tigers in the northern provinces. The lion has disappeared completely, but hyenas, cats, leopards, and chee-tahs live here, and packs of wolves invade the villages even in broad daylight. Seals, first recorded by Herodotus, are still seen in the Caspian.

Caviar, the eggs of sturgeon, is the main industry around the Caspian. Usually the fish is about twelve years old before it bears any caviar. Each fish usually has two or three kilos of eggs which have to be taken out when the sturgeon is freshly caught. There are three kinds of caviar: beluga, sevruga, and osetra. Osetra comes in degrees of golden color; only once have I seen it almost white, from an albino sturgeon. It is very rare.

Industrial pollution in the Caspian creates the present caviar scarcity, and although the fishing is controlled, widespread smuggling tends to increase as the price of caviar rises. I was told that the largest amount of sturgeon's eggs that has ever been found in one fish is eighty kilos. One can well understand why there is poaching.

Iranians love the Caspian, but I found it hard to appreciate, as the sand is a dull gray and no matter how far you walk out in the dirty water to swim it is never over your head. The air is humid and fetid beyond belief. I can only assume this humidity heals people who live in an otherwise dry climate.

As the trip from the Caspian to Tehran is so dangerous, with high mountain passes and narrow winding roads, the security people insisted that we fly back to Tehran. We returned to the Caspian often to stay with our Iranian friends who had summer homes there.

10

Iranian Women: Return to the Chador?

There are three kinds of friends, some are by tongue, some are by money and some are by love.

To Western eyes, especially those of feminists, the chador has come to represent the repression of Eastern women. I found that this notion is not necessarily true; the veil seems to be a privilege as well as a prison. A total covering, it was probably first worn to protect attractive women from becoming the spoils of war. While the veil existed in pre-Islamic times, its connection with Islam began when Mohammad encouraged its use among his wives. The veil eventually gained the same prestige that the women enjoyed as wives of the Prophet. Soon other women began to wear the veil and so the custom spread.

There is a certain status attached to the veil. For a man, it endorses his role as head of the family. For a woman, it means, among other things, that her husband can afford to protect the honor of his family from abuse. Therefore some husbands demand that their wives wear the veil.

Tribal women do not wear the veil at all, although some settled nomads have started to wear it. In the villages, during the course of their normal daily life, women who wore the veil outside their houses mixed freely with both males and females of the extended family. But it is still believed that unmarried, or unrelated, men and women should not be alone together, human nature being what it is. In days past, when women of the royal household wanted to venture out, heralds were sent to clear the streets and even to close the shops on their chosen route.

When Reza Shah came to power in 1925, he decided that the modernization of his country should involve giving rights to women. One of the first changes he worked toward was the discouragement of the wearing of the veil and the chador. In order to emphasize this, the Shah forbade members of his family to wear the chador in public.

The first break in tradition came in 1928 when Reza Shah's wife visited the shrine in Qom wearing a lighter patterned chador. She was chided by one of the religious leaders. When Reza Shah heard this, he went immediately to Qom, entered the mosque without removing his boots, and punished the priest in charge with his riding crop.

A few years later, in 1936, the Queen and two of the Princesses arrived without their chadors at a graduation of the women teachers' training college, a fitting place for this first appearance. In February 1936 the law abandoning the chador went into effect, which meant that Iran became the only Moslem country to outlaw the veil and the chador. Government officials were to be subject to discharge if their wives appeared wearing it in public.

Mrs. Gharemani, who started as my language teacher and became my friend and one of the many knowledgeable people who faithfully answered my many questions about the culture, told me with twinkling eyes that when Reza Shah outlawed the chador it was very traumatic. Her father was a member of the Majlis and Reza Shah had decreed that no member of his government was allowed to have his wife in a chador by the opening of the next session. Mrs. Gharemani told me there was an air of excitement in her house as they worked for two months, with a lot of chatter and laughter, making her mother Western clothes.

Finally the day arrived, and her mother got dressed. The carriage came to the door. But her mother was totally incapable of crossing the threshold without her chador. Her father spent an hour or more on his knees, pleading with his wife, knowing that if she did not he would lose his job. But she would not go. He resigned a few months later.

Mrs. Gharemani said that the chador was sometimes very useful. You could pass your husband in the street on the way to a rendezvous and chances are he wouldn't recognize you. And it hides anything from a receding chin to large hips, revealing only the eyes, the mirror of the soul. It covers all flesh except hands, feet, and face, and most of one's clothing. Arms must always be covered; the top of a woman's arm is considered very provocative. When a hand is needed for another purpose, the chador is disconcertingly placed between the teeth. A twist of cloth on either side of the head is essential to prevent the veil from slipping off. Traditionally all hair should be covered. It is considered tantalizing to allow some hair to show.

Sir Richard Burton, the English explorer, once called the chador the most coquettish article of women's attire. Certainly Iranian prostitutes manipulate it in a most flirtatious way; but without the proper signal a man would not dare to approach a veiled woman. If he did, he could be in trouble, because a woman's honor involves her sexual chastity. If the loss of her honor becomes public knowledge, male members of her family may feel bound to cleanse the family name. This cleansing can be extreme, even allowing the taking of the young woman's life, with no subsequent prosecution.

Under Islamic law, the husband is head and master of the household. He selects the family's residence, and because of the extended family relationship, this may well be with *his* family.

A Persian man is not used to the "nuclear" family. Few men spend time alone with their wives and children; they prefer to go out or to visit with the extended family, sometimes as often as six nights a week. When his father dies, an Iranian husband often expects his wife to become totally committed to the care and amusement of his mother. This can be especially difficult for a foreign wife when the mother is a chadori (one who wears the veil) and quite unworldly. There is also an almost universal view that anyone outside the extended family is hostile.

In many cases, the extended family tradition is kinder than a nuclear family environment; kinder because single people, women, and widows are included in all family functions. Old people are respected and surviving parents well taken care of. Moslem women also benefit from the help of the extended family while they raise children.

Still, men have most of the control. A young friend of mine discovered, a few days after the death of her husband, that she had virtually no money and no longer owned her house, and that she would not necessarily have custody of her children. She was totally at the mercy of her father-in-law. He, fortunately, was kind to her. This tradition is dying out in favor of the less charitable practices of the West. But old expectations remain and moving couples or a nuclear family to an industrial site has caused a lot of hardship and unhappiness.

The prophet Mohammad was the first to reform the status of women in Arabic culture by changing some tribal customs. Many of the laws governing marriage in Iran are derived from the Koran. Because Islam is a way of life as well as a religion, the Koran was not only a religious treatise, but also the basis for a code of civil law. Women were given inheritance rights and retained their right to dowry. Polygamy was limited to four cowives, with all wives being treated equally. But while the new polygamy law represented an improvement for Arabic women (Mohammad had married twelve wives in the twelve years following the death of Khadijeh, his wife of twenty-five years), the change was less drastic in Iran where old practices often persisted.

Many marriages are still arranged by families for economic, political, or social reasons. Often the girls are very young. In the rural areas couples may be acquainted even if they are subject to arranged marriages, but in the upper classes couples may not have met before the engagement party and would be allowed little or no contact before the wedding ceremony. Marriage is a social and not a romantic proposition.

The public baths in Iran are not only a great place for gossip but are often the only source of information about a future partner. Many a young man has sent his mother or a sister off to the baths to look over a candidate. In earlier days a beauty was required to have plump ankles. One can imagine the young man waiting impatiently for his sister's return, wondering whether her news will inspire instant longing, sad resignation, or a sudden desire to renegotiate!

Under the Pahlavi dynasty, the legal age to marry was raised to eighteen for women and twenty for men, although a court can allow an earlier marriage. Such marriage laws are hard to enforce, particularly in the rural areas where sixty percent of the population still lives in villages and eighty percent of the women are illiterate. Many men in both the cities and rural areas would prefer that their wives remain ignorant of their rights.

There is a gap between Western-oriented women and those who live a more traditional existence, not only in the rural areas but in the same city and sometimes in the same household. The sexuality of girls and even women is often used to control their lives. Sexual chastity is expected, and in order to have no misunderstanding about this even the physical exercise of girls prior to their marriage is restricted. They are not allowed to ride bicycles or do any physical exertion that might rupture the hymen. (A gynecologist told me that no physical exercise short of sitting on a picket fence would do this.) A man wants to know that the child in his wife's womb is his own, and so she must be a virgin at the time of marriage.

A *mehriyeh,* or marriage settlement—the amount is written into the contract—is a commitment by the husband to the wife. This is theoretically payable to the wife upon demand during her marriage but is traditionally demanded only upon death or divorce.

Some recent young brides told me they do not like the connotation of the *mehriyeh* as it gives them the feeling of being sold. Many forego the *mehriyeh,* often accepting a gold coin or a token in its place. Formerly, many foreign wives, who either did not or could not read the fine print on their marriage contracts, signed away their *mehriyeh* without knowing what it was.

In Iran a marriage can be performed under any of four religions: Islam, Christianity, Judaism, or Zoroastrianism. Under Iranian law, if a non-Moslem marries a Moslem, either male or female, he or she must convert to Islam. Furthermore, an Iranian woman must have permission from the government to marry an alien. Cohabitation without marriage is a felony.

Moslem law permits a man to take four wives at any one time as long as he treats them equally in every respect. For Shi'ites, temporary wives, or *sigheh,* are also legal. Sunni Moslems do not recognize the legality of these wives. While *sigheh* children are legitimate, *sigheh* spouses do not inherit from one another.

Shi'ite Moslem law does not stipulate how many *sighehs* are allowed, nor their duration. The marriage, which must be performed by a mullah, can last for one hour or for a lifetime. The parties themselves provide in their contract how long the marriage will last, and divorce is automatic at the end of this period.

Cross-cultural marriages present their own special problems, both legal and social. For example, marriage abroad is valid only if registered by both parties at an Iranian embassy or consulate. Many foreign women are unaware that their marriages are invalid if not registered and that therefore if they return to Iran their husbands can take other wives. Even if the marriage takes place in a non-Moslem church, if one of the parties is a Moslem it is subject to Moslem law when the couple returns to Iran.

Foreign women who are married to Iranians automatically become Iranian citizens when their marriage is registered in Iran. If recent attempts to change the law are successful, a foreign wife would retain her citizenship and not need her husband's permission to leave the country. (Currently no woman may leave the country without her husband's written and notarized permission. Permission may be given for one year, but without it a woman cannot even join her husband abroad.) However, if she wishes to work, she would have to apply for a work permit, which she now gets automatically as a citizen. Many American wives told me that since Iran's economic boom it has been easier to get permission to leave the country, as passports are costly and, at the time we were there, a person had to pay about $150 at each departure.

In a cross-cultural marriage, the serenity of family life often depends upon the knowledge and respect of different customs. Unlike Americans, Iranians greet everyone when they enter a room and stand when an older person joins them. Such small but important traditions have sometimes become a bone of contention when a foreign wife enters a family.

One extremely attractive American woman unfolded for me the evolution of her eighteen-year marriage to an Iranian. Her story is typical of many Western women who are eager to marry and who overlook the different laws and customs they are committing themselves to in Iran. She recalled with nostalgia her mother's insistence that she first talk with the embassy consul. She did, but as she now admits, nothing would have changed her mind, and she really didn't pay any attention. Arriving in Iran she found that her father-in-law had four wives, all wearing the veil, and a number of children. As in most Eastern marriages, she married a family as well as a man. According to local custom, the new couple moved in with the husband's family and lived with them for many years. The American wife learned the language, and the family was very kind to her in spite of her Western peculiarities. But she had to deal constantly with a lack of privacy and her husband's almost schizophrenic loyalty to his Western wife and his Iranian family. She contended the situation worsened as they grew older.

Many women have married Iranians abroad and lived with their husbands in the West. The spouses seem totally Westernized, but sometimes after many years of marriage, perhaps influenced by Iran's economic development and need to bring trained Iranians back home, they may suddenly announce they are returning to Iran. As one wife put it, "All Iranian men are actors. They have the total ability to take on the role of the country they are in. They become French, English, American, and German. But when they return home their reversion is equally complete."

The Family Protection Act of 1967 and its 1975 amendments resulted in many improvements for women in Iran and modernized the interpretations of Islamic traditions. Before the Family Protection Act, a wife could be divorced without her knowledge. Any day a knock could come at the door and she could receive a piece of paper saying she had been divorced. It struck me as an insecure way of life.

Now, if a court grants a man permission to take a second wife—which it may if his first wife gives him written permission to remarry and the court is sure that he has the physical and financial resources to maintain both wives—he has to support the first one until she remarries; she may leave his house or stay as she pleases. Alimony used to be paid for only a hundred days, or until it was certain the wife was not pregnant, and the *mehriyeh* was important for subsequent support. (If a wealthy woman wants the divorce, she must support her ex-husband until he remarries or finds another means of support!)

Things have changed. There are now fourteen recognized situations where men and women can go to court and ask for a divorce. These are the fairly valid reasons that one would expect: incompatibility, drug addiction, desertion, disease, reluctance to cohabit, childlessness, or the taking of a second wife without the court's permission. To obtain a divorce both parties must appear in court. (Under Islamic law a woman's testimony in any legal proceeding is worth half that of a man. Because women are considered to have less reason than men, two women must testify to every one man to be credible.) The physical presence of both parties is mandatory since some husbands pressure their wives to divorce by beating them. A husband has to produce the body and stand her up in court, and a women's organization provides a social worker who will go to court with a wife—if she knows that she may ask for one. But there are still many judges whom we would call "unreconstructed."

Upon divorce the husband used to be given automatic custody of the children after they passed the earliest years of childhood. Now the court decides custody, but usually awards the children to the Moslem partner, particularly if the mother is a foreigner who plans to leave the country. After divorce a woman may leave the country without her husband's permission, but the children need it until they are eighteen.

Up to early 1979, at the time of the revolution, women were making gains in other areas, too. More and more Iranian women were becoming better educated. A woman's right to education is established under Islamic law, but many Islamic societies ignore this. In his efforts to modernize Iran, Reza Shah introduced compulsory education for girls as well as boys. In 1934 he ordered that women be admitted to medical school at Tehran University. Reza Shah also tried to raise the literacy rate, which was particularly low among women. The task was taken up by his son, who in a 1963 announcement made fighting illiteracy one of the six original points of the White Revolution. Today perhaps fifty percent of the population is literate, but the rate is still lower for women than for men.

Religious customs did not allow parents to hand over daughters to male teachers, so the Shah's Literacy Corps was augmented by a Corps of Women. These groups of reading, writing, and arithmetic teachers were among the most successful of the Shah's reforms.

Frances Gray, the American head of Damavand College for Girls, came to me with a delegation of Iranian educators and asked me to join the Board of Trustees of the American-supported college. I hesitated, as I knew it would be time-consuming, but I was so impressed by the Iranian women that I agreed. They became my good friends and serving on the board awakened me to Iran's many education problems, particularly the education of women.

Dr. Gray believed that the most important and immediate need was to improve the self-image of young women. Living in a completely male-dominated society, they lacked the self-confidence to generate their own ideas, research papers, or even understand or interpret the great books. She told me it was fearfully hard to break the accepted patterns of their lives.

While parents were supportive and allowed their daughters to take whatever courses were offered, they often objected to swimming classes. When I asked one of the parents why (it couldn't be modesty, since the girls were probably going to be with other women in the public baths), he said he was afraid that the next step would be that his daughter would want to be on a public beach.

We were happy that we had the support of so many community leaders, and also happy that so many of the girls succeeded and went on to study for higher degrees in America or Europe. During the earlier riots when every other college and university closed, Damavand stayed open and suffered from no strikes at least until the riots of 1978. In 1979 the college had two thousand applications for two hundred places.

The Iranian women's struggle to be accepted as part of the work force is a struggle against tradition. At the time Dick and I were in Iran, the number of professionally trained women was increasing and many women were employed in areas other than agriculture and domestic labor. But even Western-educated families continued to oppose office work for women, though members of their family might be university graduates, career-minded, and needed in the work force. Prejudices remained, and some men said that women office workers had not yet learned to be responsible and were apt to go off to get their hair done in the middle of the day. Many middle-class mothers did prefer to have their daughters work for American businesses rather than in offices with Iranian men. They believed they would be better treated; the break with tradition was not quite as shameful under those conditions.

At the time I was in Iran, working women did get some help in coping with their birth and child-care responsibilities. By law women had to receive equal pay and many women were also entitled to have their childbirth expenses paid by their employer's insurance. Women were given generous maternity leave and were paid a full salary and their jobs were held for them during this time. In a large factory conglomerate that I revisited on a return trip to Tehran, a day-care center was being planned by the industrialist's wife, herself a businesswoman. The factory employed many women. Its owner was a devout Moslem who had already built a mosque for his workers and seemed genuinely concerned about the welfare of his people.

Despite these advances, the Family Protection Act has in one way restricted a woman's liberty to engage in the occupation of her choice. The Act carries forward the 1926 Civil Code provision which allows a man to legally stop his wife from working if he finds that his wife's job offends his or his family's position. While a court must first rule on the husband's complaint, once an employer receives a court order to discharge the woman, it must do so immediately.

Contradictions also persist in women's property rights. Islamic law permits a woman to own property with no ties. In this she is better off than many women in America, where property laws vary from state to state. However, the present laws of inheritance have come down unchanged from Mohammad through the Koran. If a woman dies first and leaves no children, her husband inherits one-half of her property; with children, he will inherit only one-quarter. At the same time a wife inherits only one-eighth of her husband's property, excluding land. If there is more than one wife, that portion is shared among them. Sons inherit twice as much as daughters, and if the deceased leaves parents, they inherit one-third.

This reaffirmation of the male-dominated society is also encountered in religion. According to the order of the religious leaders, if a woman starts her period while she is performing *namaz,* the prayer is ruined. However, under Islamic jurisprudence a husband may not formally repudiate his wife during menses. The fact that a woman is "polluted" when she is menstruating is often given as the final argument that she cannot participate fully in religious life. She may become a religious teacher but not a spiritual leader.

In recent times Iranian women have begun to assume at least secular leadership roles. In 1963 the Shah granted women of legal age the right to vote and to be elected to the Majlis and the Senate. One of my friends from a northern province was elected to the Parliament then and has been a member ever since. There was strong opposition from the religious leaders and women were harassed in the streets. But by 1973 there were more women in the Iranian Parliament than in our Congress and there were numerous women in top government jobs, including one in the cabinet—the Minister of Education. After the revolution, she was imprisoned, then shot.

The vast new wealth in Iran has also had an effect on the lives of some women. Wealthy Iranian women can spend freely on fabulous jewelry, French designer clothes—one of the first signs of prosperity in a newly developing country—and education abroad for their children. Extremely intelligent and usually very generous, they give large donations to their favorite charity, but, except for a few dedicated women, rarely give that charity an hour of their time. Many play cards in the morning and siesta in the afternoon. Prior to the revolution, they were beginning to take jobs, start businesses, or train for a profession.

But not all of them have so eagerly accepted the influence of the West. Since the veil is not always a sign of oppression, the effort to have it discarded has had many setbacks. In the early seventies, women sat beside men in university classes, but gradually the women started to wear the chador again and then moved away and sat separately. They did not want their friends to think they were inciting the young men. Did this reversion to the chador signify stronger religious beliefs? A sign of dissatisfaction encouraged by the religious leaders? A remonstrance against the unattractive aspects of the freedom witnessed in the West?

I asked a young, good-looking, sociable girl whom I had known for some time why she had started to wear a chador again. She said she found her way of doing things had been wrong according to her religion. Men were looking at her differently: with desire. She felt she had been encouraging her brothers to be libertines.

The return to the chador was also, in part, a reaction to the "Western decadence" many people thought the royal family was imposing on them, in direct opposition to their religious training. Revealing billboards had appeared, sometimes advertising Western cosmetic products. Sexy films were imported or shown on television, and their own press started to pay attention to and promote young Iranian women singers. Night clubs and gambling had become popular, and brothers were returning from school abroad with tales of the permissive society in modern America. Many young women told me they did not think Westerners were any happier because of this permissiveness.

At any rate, as I came to understand that Islam is not only a religion, but a way of life, I appreciated more and more the Iranian woman's problem: How can she respond to a strong religious faith while at the same time participate in the development of her country?

11

Islam as a Way of Life

A true spring is that which gives out water of itself.

In Mashhad, a city in the northeast of Iran, lies the tomb of the eighth Imam. Visited by millions of pilgrims every year, the shrine was built during the reign of the Timurid dynasty and the adjacent mosque was built by Gowhar Shad, the wife of Shah Rokh, in 1414. The area surrounding the mosque and the shrine is sacrosanct to believers, and in recent years a great deal of ill feeling was generated as the small shops and traditional way of life around the shrine area were moved to make way for wide boulevards and other expressions of modernization.

The village of Sanabad became Mashhad, "the place of martyrdom," when the eighth Imam died there in 813 A.D. He is said to have eaten a poisoned grape. Mashhad lies on the main route to Afghanistan, and was the capital of Persia in 1722. A city with a harsh climate of extreme heat and cold, it has a beautiful setting of bordering mountains and long avenues of pine trees, but its buildings are undistinguished except for the shrine and the mosque.

For many years foreign travelers have tried in vain to visit the shrine, and only recently have a very few even been allowed in the vicinity. Dick and I were dying to go. Our chance came when the governor of the province of Khorasan invited Dick to Mashhad on an official visit. The governor suggested we come as soon as possible because a long religious holiday was about to begin the following week. Mashhad would be even more crowded than usual, and we certainly wouldn't be able to visit the shrine.

We flew down one afternoon, a six-hundred-mile journey that kept us in constant sight of the Alborz Mountains. Descending through a pass into Mashhad, we could see some of the black tribal tents of the Turkomans and tribesmen striding across the foothills with their sheep and goats.

That night we dined in splendor at the Shah's palace, a small one-story building surrounded by trees and a garden he was restoring. Although he was not in residence, we stayed there at the Shah's invitation as a courtesy to the American ambassador. We dined on *fesenjan,* which is duck with walnuts in pomegranate juice, and *bagali-polow,* a rice cooked with lima beans. We finished with *shakte* melon, a local product so sweet it is surely a fruit from paradise. Dick told the governor that we were very interested in Iran's religions, and that we would give anything to be able to visit the Imam's tomb.

The next day the governor general came to call on us and welcomed us to his province. He told us that he had arranged for us to go to the shrine, and he would send a car for us the next morning.

I couldn't sleep. I had read so many times about travelers waiting and waiting for permission to go and finally being turned away. I was sure something would happen and we wouldn't be allowed in either. I got up early and wandered around the garden, calming my nerves with handfuls of large, luscious black cherries. Finally, late in the morning, the governor's car arrived to drive us to his mansion. We drank tea at midday and met a few of the governor's associates.

We had to leave separately, according to sex. The time, early afternoon, would be the least crowded. We drove along a broad avenue lined with trees, but as we drove toward the shrine I began to feel apprehensive. Religious fanatics have been known to attack not only nonbelievers, but also some of their own for not being dressed conservatively enough. My Persian teacher had told me of being accosted in the mosque at Qom because her arms were visible under her chador.

A street scene in Qom, famed for its many mullahs. (JAMES CUNNINGHAM)

But as we drew nearer the sense of awe that I always feel when I approach a shrine took over, and some of my fears melted away. The majesty of the minarets and domes as they reached toward the heavens, the glory of the colors, the gilt and the blue faience domes almost overwhelmed me. On this day the beige, dark blue, and white of the tiles of Naskh and Kufic writing proclaiming the message of the Koran were sublime under a bright, cloudless sky.

Dressed in somber, long-sleeved clothes, the governor's wife and I stopped near the courtyard and put on chadors. It is difficult to keep it from slipping off one's hair unless you twist it in a certain way on the side of your head, and I had worked hard at learning to hold it in my teeth as many of the women do. We left the car some distance away, and as we walked toward the great courtyard I was conscious of a few curious eyes looking at me; I kept my head bowed. I was probably not wearing my chador in the same relaxed fashion that Iranian women do. The area was crowded with pilgrims, many of them very poor, and some who had taken days to travel there. All were quiet and seemed to be contemplating this moving experience. I was sure that for many just being there was the dream of a lifetime.

Adjacent to the compound was a large complex of religious buildings: the shrine, mosques, and *madresehs,* or religious schools. There was also a library and museum. The shrine and the mosques were cleared and the floors scrubbed and washed down three times a day, the interior was then sprayed with rose water. Nevertheless, the buildings smelled of many human beings. As we moved slowly across the courtyard into the halls, all the marble floors were jammed with kneeling pilgrims fingering their prayer beads, or *tasbih,* as they murmured their appeals. In front of each person lay a Koran and a small flat man-made clay stone, or *mohr,* to rest their foreheads on as they bowed their heads.

We picked our way through the crowd. I saw my husband and walked by him three times, but he did not recognize me in my chador. I was swept along with a group receiving lighted candles. Not knowing what to do, I put out my hand, but the donor glanced up and met my eye. He passed me over. He knew green eyes and auburn hair were not dark enough for a Persian.

I was scared that I would lose the governor's wife, or that I would tread on somebody's precious possession, or stumble over a body, or drop my veil. I was torn between a longing to participate in this rare experience and an uncomfortable feeling that, as a nonbeliever, I was in a place where I was not welcome.

We continued to walk, passing slowly through a chamber of glittering mirrors and tile that sparkled with the light from large crystal chandeliers. As we entered the actual shrine, the sense of peace began to shatter. Grillwork in silver surrounds the tomb itself, and some pilgrims had roped themselves there as if to transmit the believed power of the Imam to themselves. Many had brought their sick and troubled relatives. All of them were wailing.

The people seemed to want to touch their shrines; their fervor and emotion was impressive. As a witness, I watched the wailing and prostration, the hurtling of coins and even jewelry, the padlocks and pieces of cloth they tied to the grillwork while the people made their commitment, or *nazr.* In this emotional moment, I thought I envied the belief of these people that the Imam had the power to intercede on judgment day and to perform miracles. But their behavior seemed to me more a reminder of the material world and its sadness, difficulties, and frustrations, for the beseeching pilgrims seemed to far outweigh the ones giving thanks. (Unlike many people, Iranians do carry out their commitments—their promise to build a shrine if a child is made well, or to

Me and a friend dressed in chadors.

sacrifice twenty sheep if a troubled father feels better, is usually kept.)

Dick and I met back at the governor's residence. While he continued his talks with the governor I went to visit the house of an Iranian friend. Nobody was there except the mother of the family, who had withdrawn from the modern world. I talked with her briefly, sitting beside her on a cushion in her private quarters. Then I took some grapes offered me from a large platter of fruit and went out to the garden. It was peaceful and quiet, so different from the seething emotional mob inside the shrine.

I couldn't leave Mashhad without another pilgrimage—to Nishapur, the home of Omar Khayyam. Born around 1048, Khayyam is the best known of Persian poets in the West, undoubtedly because of Edward FitzGerald's translation of the *Rubaiyat*. But with a sense of sadness, I had already discovered that he was not Iran's most beloved poet. In moments of spontaneous recitation, it was Sa'di, Rumi, Hafez, and Ferdowsi who they preferred to quote. To his contemporaries Khayyam was known as a philosopher and mathematician rather than as a poet. He compiled a set of astronomical tables forming the base of a new solar calendar that even today experts say is more accurate than the Gregorian calendar. It has an error of only one day in five thousand years.

Khayyam spoke of Avicenna, the great Moslem sage and philosopher, born a century before in Bokhara, as his great master. A follower of Aristotelian philosophy, Khayyam is known for his treatises on algebra and his work with other astronomers in constructing an observatory at Esfahan. Considered by many to be a mystic, a Sufi, or even an agnostic, his thoughts on life and death and creation may be the reason Islamic theologians have encouraged the study of other poets.

We drove southwest through a sparsely populated area on the edge of the desert, below the steep southern slopes of the Alborz Mountains. This was part of Iran's fertile crescent, and here fruit trees and flowers grew everywhere in proliferation, although they looked unkempt to the Western eye.

Nishapur's development dramatizes for me much of the history of the area. Founded in Sasanian times by Shapur I (240–71 A.D.), Nishapur grew as a center of fire worship and trade. Through the centuries it was a trading center for silk, carpets, spices, dyes, and turquoise from the local mines. Since the caravans stopped there it was also a marketplace for produce and for changing caravans. The most beautiful of all Islamic pottery came from Nishapur.

After the Islamic invasion it became the capital of Khorasan and an intellectual center of learning with thirteen large libraries and a university where students from all parts of the known world could come to study. In 1219, Genghis Khan's forces destroyed Nishapur and slaughtered every living thing.

Now that we had made these two visits, it seemed natural to think of another Islamic journey—the one to Mecca. To understand this greatest of all pilgrimages, you must first know the principles of belief of the Islamic faith. The five major principles for twelver Shi'ites are: *towhid,* monotheism, or the uniqueness of God; *nabovvat,* the prophetic mission of Mohammad, sent by God as his last Prophet; *imamat,* Mohammad named his son-in-law Ali as his successor (this principle separates the Shi'a from the Sunnis); *adl,* justice (God is just); *ma'ad,* upon death or the day of reckoning you will be judged by God.

The eight subsidiary principles are *namaz,* prayers; *ruzeh,* fasting; *hajj,* the pilgrimage; *khoms* and *zakat,* taxation and support of the poor; *amr be ma'ruf,* the duty to force people to do the right thing; *nahy az monker,* the duty to prevent people from doing the wrong thing; and *jehad,* holy war.

If you are willing to observe all these principles, you declare *ashhad,* or the confession of faith, when you perform your *namaz.* This is expressed in the formula, "There is no God but Allah, and Mohammad is his Prophet." The Shi'a add "and Ali is his Assistant."

In Iran the five ritual daily prayers, or *namaz,* in most instances are performed on three occasons, with the noon and afternoon and the sunset and evening prayers being said together. When I traveled out in the country I tried to stop at the appropriate time so that my driver and guard could say their prayers, but we could not always find a stream for them to perform their mandatory ablutions.

The second obligation is the fast from sunrise to sunset during the month of Ramazan. You may be excused from this fast if you are physically unfit or on a journey. If you do not know the hour of sunset, it is decreed that you tell it by whether you can distinguish a white thread from a black one. Ramazan, even if you are not fasting, is a time for contemplation. From first light until sunset you should abstain from food, drink, tobacco, and sexual intercourse. There should be no parties, and merrymaking and conversation should be subdued in public places at this time.

The required taxation of twenty percent of income and voluntary alms to the poor are heeded, and with the new wealth in Iran alms and taxation paid to the religious leaders have made the religious centers and schools and the religious leaders extremely wealthy and therefore powerful.

The *hajj,* the once in a lifetime pilgrimage to Mecca, in Saudia Arabia, is not made by all Moslems, but it is something they all aspire to and most manage to make once. To many it is the culmination of years of planning and saving. Most men attach the title of "Haji" to their name after completing the pilgrimage.

The *hajj* is also a way of achieving social integration. Through the centuries, Moslems from all parts of the world have met every year and exchanged ideas and goods. Through this, many have come to realize the vastness of the Islamic world and to know its other parts and peoples. This was probably true to a greater extent in the past than nowadays, with improved communications.

Although the *hajj* is obligatory under Moslem law it may only be taken when certain conditions are fulfilled: You must be a Moslem, healthy and physically strong; the road must be safe; and you must be able to meet the financial commitments. These include both your own expenses and the support of your family, if necessary, while you are away. If you are a nonbeliever you are not allowed to visit Mecca. You are not even allowed to fly over it. I only know of one nonbeliever who has made the trip. Dark complected and fluent in Arabic, he was nevertheless recognized when he stood up to relieve himself. All Easterners squat.

In the past Shi'ites have had difficulties on the pilgrimage at the hands of the Wahhabis, the sect of the ruling royal family of Saudi Arabia. They differ on the calendar and many of the rituals. An Iranian pilgrim was beheaded in Mecca and for some years the relations between the two countries were severed. The Shah himself had to intervene to gain safe conduct for the Iranian pilgrims.

The obligation of *jehad* is a collective community defense of the tradition of Islam. The other pillars of faith are obligations to individuals. The term *jehad,* or exertion of struggle, is a concept to further the spread of the belief in Allah and the Islamic tradition, and to guard the Islamic world. Often called a holy war, it does not necessarily mean exertion through war or fighting. It may be a form of religious mission carried out by peaceful means. In fact, *jehad* by means of the sword, or in modern times guns, is a rare phenomenon in Islamic history. The jurists of Islamic law have agreed that a believer may fulfill his obligations of *jehad* by his heart, his tongue, his hands or his sword. The war may be waged with any of these against unbelievers or enemies of the faith. It may well include the war of an individual against himself and his passions.

In addition to the principles there are many intricate laws of the religion. All acts of daily life are according to Islamic laws. The two terms that you hear most often are *haram,* or forbidden, and *halal,* permitted. There is some flexibility but, for instance, bacon is always *haram* even if you are dying of hunger.

It is the believers' obligation to learn the laws for problems they face daily. There are eleven kinds of impurities, including wine, beer, and all alcoholic beverages, dogs, semen, fermented grapes or grape juice, and fish that do not have scales. Hashish is pure, but its use is forbidden. Those who openly deny God and have no religion are impure. This accounts for the special utensils you may be served with in a cafe, particularly in the bazaar where there are many conservative believers. (The only article ever stolen from me in the embassy was a tiny Koran. Was it because I was a nonbeliever or because of its value? I will never know.)

There are five types of pure water to be used for ablutions before prayers. Among these are rain, well, or spring water—a small amount in a clean vessel. There are no stipulations for the condition of cleanliness of the water. Using gold or silver vessels is *haram,* but this applies only to the home. When a person evacuates his body he must not face Mecca, nor have his back directly toward it. After urinating the genital area does not become purified before praying unless water is used to clean it. There is always a hose of water in every latrine in Iran, even where there are the most modern, Western-style toilets.

The rules for cleansing or ablutions before *namaz* are numerous. They even cover all possibilities of menstruation. If a woman starts her period during *namaz,* the prayer is ruined. The fact that a woman is impure during menstruation and that she may not say her prayers at that time is one of the reasons given that a woman will never reach the highest level of religious leadership. The rules for charity are also set down to the last camel, and for buying and selling. The laws against the charging of interest were one of the reasons the Iranian banks were burned during the riots at the end of 1978.

The Shi'as recognize the practice of *taqiyeh,* a difficult concept to translate, but perhaps camouflaging one's beliefs or intentions comes close to it. This term may have originated in order to permit one to mislead an adversary about religion, thus to protect oneself from religious persecution. In the days of Sunni reprisal against the Shi'a, *taqiyeh* was an alteration of truth allowed in religious practices to protect oneself from bodily harm. Dissimulation has been used extensively by Sufi mystics.

I find the concept of *taqiyeh* not only interesting, but important for foreigners to understand. Iranians try to protect themselves by giving away as little as possible while they learn as much as they can about everyone else. They consider it religiously wrong or desecrating to reveal true beliefs to nonbelievers. Even written texts, particularly of mystics, have become secret in order to hide their real intentions and because Iranians want to limit knowledge of their beliefs to an intellectual and spiritual elite. Nikkie Keddie, Professor of Persian Studies at the University of California, told me that few scholars have written about this concept but they recognize its importance, because of dissimulation by Iranian scholars and its effect on the study of their work.

Foreigners do not often get the opportunity to see the *ta'ziyeh,* or passion plays, the only indigenous drama of the Islamic world. They take place during the month of Moharram, the month of mourning for the Shi'ite martyrs. When we went, the acting was crude but dramatic, and was performed on a round central stage that was not raised and had no exit for the performers or their horses. But it was a powerful performance that lasted about two hours, and often, I was told, lasts much longer.

The Iranians, even the Empress, who was attending that night, were totally and emotionally involved in the performance. Many were sobbing loudly. The performance was a reenactment of the death of the third Imam of Shi'a Moslems, Hoseyn, son of Ali and grandson of the Prophet, and his death on the plain at Karbala, Iraq. On the tenth day of Moharram in 680 A.D., on the orders of the Caliph Yazid, an army surrounded Imam Hoseyn and his small party of followers. In the play, even the murder of his infant son was dramatically depicted. But Hoseyn had sacrificed himself to ensure the sanctity of his faith and the battle at Karbala represents emotionally and dramatically that might is not necessarily right and that in the end truth and faith will prevail. The *mohr,* or small tablet Iranians rest their heads on when they pray, is made of clay from the Karbala plain.

There is an almost total identification of the Iranian people with their martyrs and their suffering. Their pain and punishment are very much a part of their culture. In every town and village, the tenth day of Ashura is commemorated by ceremonies in which men move through the streets and bazaars in groups, flagellating themselves with chains to a rhythmic beat. They hold the chains in their hands and swing them onto their backs. As we arrived back at the American compound, we could hear them coming down Roosevelt Avenue. We listened to the intermittent rhythmic clanking of the chains all evening, and eventually we walked to the gate and stood in the shadows to watch. The flagellants work themselves into a fervid hypnotic state and appear to feel no pain. In the past they have been known to insert metal objects into their skin. It is best that foreigners or nonbelievers are not on the streets during this period. Religious ecstasy can cause strange incidents.

12

Poetry and Persian Gardens

To talk of life's enjoyments is by itself half the pleasure.

Each month I lived in Iran I became aware of something new within its culture, and I realized that Dick, who always uses his hands expressively when he talks, was absorbing the different culture too when he explained to me a conversation he had with an Iranian. He ran his hand from left to right to demonstrate what he had said and from right to left, the way the Persian script runs, when he repeated what the Iranian had said.

Conversation in Iran is seldom brief. There are certain formalities that must be observed. Fond of excessive politeness, Iranians use flowery language even in telephone greetings and farewells. They believe a direct no is impolite. As a result it takes practice to understand what an Iranian sometimes intends to say. "Yes" may mean "yes, yes," "maybe yes," or "no yes." There are certain Persian words that define cultural practices. *Ta'arof* is excessive politeness and *parti-bazi* is the use of influence through friends or acquaintances. A gift given to thank an individual, or to get something desired in return, is *pish-kesh.* But none of these terms have the bad connotation of *reshveh,* a bribe, although one of Sa'di's admonitions is that as long as an affair can be arranged with gold, it is not necessary to endanger life. All these are recognized from the poorest to the richest, from the villages to the palaces.

We sometimes came close to making mistakes. John Evans, my husband's staff aide, warned him just in time at a U.S. trade fair when he was about to place a cowboy hat on the head of the Prime Minister. A popular Persian symbol for cheating someone is to put a hat on his head.

It is very rewarding and exciting when you discover you can read the street signs and then the newspaper headlines. Perhaps realizing my eagerness to learn, the servants started to leave messages for me and would hide behind a door, laughing while they watched me trying to decipher the Persian handwriting. In Persian there are three vowels written and three that are not written; there is a lot of room for guess work when you first learn to read.

I gathered a few friends together, and we started a Persian poetry class taught by Professor Jerome Clinton. Jerry was generous and patient with his time, and he introduced us to new fields of Persian culture. Much of the poetry had first been translated into English by Persian-speaking officers of the East India Company. Written over the last thousand years, the best of the Persians is revealed in the odes and lyrics of Hafez and Rumi and the narratives of Ferdowsi and Sa'di, the last and perhaps the best known of all; he was a poet who became the moralizing master of popular philosophy.

Hafez, Sa'di, and Rumi were Sufis, as was Jami, as well as some of Persia's most famous theologians and philosophers. The Sufis are the mystics of Islam who try to reach union with God while in this life. The life of purity and virtue, the love of God, and the appreciation of beauty that characterize Sufism have always been exalted ideals for Persian souls. Sufism has harbored the spiritual life within the Islamic world since the origin of the Islamic revelation and has played an especially important role in the history of Persia.

In the last few years the word *Sufi* has become a part of Western language. In fact, Sufism has been on the increase during the past few decades as can be seen by the large number of *khaneqahs,* or Sufi centers started recently all over the West. But in the East the word is not used quite so glibly. It is not something you decide to become overnight.

Rather, it is another dimension of being that can evolve in the lives of both rich and poor.

In our poetry class we read with great enthusiasm a poem by the poetess Foruq Farrokhzad, who unhappily was killed in an automobile accident at the age of thirty-two. Although classical Persian poetry is known to most Iranians, the poetry of Farrokhzad and other young modern writers was beginning to gain a following. As women are rarely mentioned in books on Islam, Farrokhzad should be remembered for her double breakthrough. She was herself a great admirer of Rumi's *Masnavi* poems.

One member of our class, Julie Samii, was born an American, married an Iranian, and had lived in Iran for twenty years. Since she was already fluent in the language, we inspired her to work on original translations of Rumi's poetry. She also created a sign language for the deaf in Persian.

Julie inspired me to continue to study, and to start to translate some children's stories from *Kalila va Dimna,* a collection of animal fables. Originally from India, they had been translated from the ancient Pahlavi language into Arabic and then into Persian. Many of them are as familiar to Iranians as Aesop's fables are to us.

Folk literature, both ancient and new, flourishes in Iran. I began work on translating folk stories that were collected from across the country through radio appeals for stories, handed down through families orally, and otherwise unrecorded. These had not been translated before, and although they are often long and repetitive, they help you understand rural life, particularly the superstitions and belief in evil spirits that continue today.

I learned much from the Court Minister, Amir Assadollah Alam. Traveling with him made me aware of many of the old customs and traditions that were still in use. One weekend we went to Birjand with Alam and his wife, Malektaj. They had invited Dick and me for a visit to his ancestral home in Birjand, Khorasan Province, near the eastern border of Iran. Alam, a true aristocrat and a member of one of the fine old families of Persia, was a statesman who enjoyed the Shah's special trust. He served his government in many capacities, including head of Pahlavi University, Prime Minister, and leader of the Mardom party. He had also spearheaded the Shah's controversial land-reform program.

His was an arranged marriage. He delighted in relating the story of being called by his father and being told that the time had come for him to marry. Young and occupied with other things, he agreed, thinking his father meant sometime in the future. Not at all. He was to play tennis with the young lady that very day, and they were to be married the following week!

Alam was the Amir, or he who gives command, of a large area in Birjand. Under the land reform, villages that his family had owned for generations were given to the people, but the Baluchi tribespeople and the villagers of that vast area still regarded him as their head, or *khan.* He still recognized the ancient tradition of the right of petition, and added to all his other duties was the time-consuming task of seeing poor people who came to his home or stood alongside the road in Khorasan to present their petitions as he passed. He would always stop for them. He needed no security guards there. The Baluchi tribesmen themselves guarded him.

When Dick and I arrived at Alam's ancestral home, the driveway was strewn with beautiful Persian rugs. The Mercedes cars drove onto them and parked there. The house was set in gently rolling, sparsely populated hills. Alam's property included acres of fruit trees and vines with grapes of every size and description. The main house reminded me of George Washington's home at Mount Vernon, with small but well-proportioned rooms and many outbuildings. It had no bathrooms, but it did have large kitchens and cooking facilities.

Alam's grandmother was widowed at eighteen. His father, though only two at the time, was raised by servants in the main house. As far as he knew his mother never entered the main house. Attached to the house was a low-columned building, a pavilion with *a'ineh-kari,* or mosaic mirrored walls, and many carpets and cushions. It had no furniture.

Each evening, in a pavilion away from the main house, Alam's father met a different wife, selected and sent there by his mother. His mother lived in a house connected to the pavilion, but on the other side. Every morning he came to have breakfast with her, and as further evidence of the matriarchal society, visitors and emissaries came to see her first before seeing her son. Beyond her house was the *andarun,* or harem. Here the wives and the concubines lived with their children. The various buildings had door knockers divided into two parts. Each part made a different sound so that the woman occupant of the house could tell if a male or female was calling. If the knocker indicated a male, she would know not to open the door without her veil on.

The door of an *andarun,* or harem, has two knockers—one for male callers, the other for female callers—which made different sounds so that the answering woman would know whether or not to wear her veil when she opened the door.

Near the old *andarum* we sat on Persian rugs shaded by a grove of trees, moving occasionally to pick a ripe pomegranate. The pomegranate, or "apple with many seeds," grows on a small shrub or tree not more than fifteen feet high. It was first cultivated in Mesopotamia about 2000 B.C. With four hundred to seven hundred seeds per fruit, it also represents another biblical allegory—the unity of many under a single authority. In areas where medicine is scarce, it combats dysentery, and a paste of the leaves is said to soothe conjunctivitis. But I am unclear as to why it became a symbol of chastity.

There is an art to eating a pomegranate. After picking a ripe one from a tree, you fondle it, gently squeezing and systematically rotating it. When it is softened you make one small hole and gently drink the juice that you have encouraged the seeds to give up. Alam persuaded his guests to try, but one guest forgot he was in a tranquil Eastern garden and squeezed too hard, confirming that pomegranate juice makes an excellent dye.

Sitting on Persian cushions under an arbor of trees, the rugs spread around us, we recited Persian poetry and listened to stories of the past. A gently flowing stream added to the feeling of cool peacefulness.

At the end of the day, Dick and I enjoy a brief respite in the garden of the embassy residence before resuming our official duties at evening functions.

Lie down beside the flowing stream
and see life passing by and know
that of the world's transient nature
this one sign is enough for us.
                    —Hafez
              fourteenth century

To Westerners a Persian garden looks unkempt; it is in no sense manicured. I found it had a tranquilizing effect on me. In our own garden at the residence I had no desire to pull a weed. The whole design was restful, with groves of pines and sycamores standing tall between the cooling turquoise-painted water courses. Lovely, bright green grass grew even under the tall trees. (Dr. Tom Soderstrom from the Smithsonian, who stayed with us on his way home from Laos where he had been studying bamboo, told me the sycamore trees in our garden were Platanus orientalis, the same ornamental species of the plane tree under which Hypocrates had first administered the oath to medical students in ancient Greece.)

Occasionally there would be a wonderful free afternoon to spend at home, sometimes just sitting and listening to the Hoopoe birds, the colorful black and white crested birds that mythology tells us carried the messages between Solomon and the Queen of Sheba, or watching the three bright green parrots that came every day at the cocktail hour. (It has been said these birds divided their time unilaterally between the Russian, the British, and the American compounds.) The ancient Greek historians wrote that Cyrus the Great called his garden *paridaeza,* or round wall. From this has come our word *paradise.* Small, large, humble, or luxuriant, the Persian garden is always surrounded by a wall. Even in remote desert areas, it is never without trees and water, the symbols of life.

Ours had something else—a stately peak of the Alborz Mountains that seemed to rise from the end of the garden itself. Snowcapped from October to the end of July, this mountain had become my own. Nothing affected it, not Islam, not the Shah and his opponents, certainly not the world's political changes. In a changing world, it stood steadfast and strong and reassuring. It was always there.

13

Oil and Nomad Hospitality

In the desert even an odd shoe is a gift from God.

Because Dick was ambassador to Iran at the time the Shah dramatically raised the price of his country's oil—a controversial action that has since affected the entire world—I think it would be worthwhile for me to discuss it here.

In 1908 the first commercial oil deposit in Iran was discovered by an Englishman at Masjed-e Soleyman in southwest Iran. In the previous century, Iranians had tried without success to enlist American help in the exploration of their minerals. In 1883 the American minister, Samuel Benjamin, reported to Washington that Iran, in its anxiety to counteract Anglo-Russian domination, would welcome American capital to exploit the untapped wealth of "coal, lead, copper, and petroleum." But our government remained indifferent to these economic possibilities, and petroleum was not mentioned again in dispatches for many years.

In the absence of the United States, other countries, particularly Britain, the Netherlands, and France, moved in to exploit the oil. They were joined by the huge American petroleum companies after World War II.

By the summer of 1973 worldwide demand for oil was overtaking capacity and prices had begun to rise. On July 31 an agreement was reached in which Iran completed the nationalization of her oil industry after seventy-two years of foreign control and operation of the principal Iranian oil fields. The foreign consortium that had managed the fields became a service contractor to the National Iranian Oil Company and its members simply purchasers of Iran's oil.

With the beginning of the Arab-Israeli War on October 6, 1973, the West became nervous about the supply of oil. On October 16, ministers of the six OPEC countries of the Persian Gulf met in Kuwait and fixed the price of Persian Gulf crude oil, wresting from the oil companies the last remnant of their control over oil prices. On October 17 the oil ministers of the Organization of Arab Petroleum Exporting Countries (OAPEC), of which Iran is not a member, met and announced an embargo on oil shipments to the United States and the Netherlands and a program of monthly cuts in oil production. This was the first effective use of oil as a weapon. By November, buyers were scrambling madly for crude oil supplies. Spot market prices soared. A substantial quantity of Iranian oil was auctioned off at prices as high as $17 a barrel, over eight times the price it had been a few months before.

The pricing of oil at the time was extremely complex. The simplest "price" for purposes of comparison is the average amount paid by major companies for "Iranian Light," then Iran's major export crude. This average price was about $1.80 per barrel in late 1972, rose to almost $2.00 at the beginning of 1973, and to about $3.80 following the October 16 OPEC meeting.

The Shah was determined to raise the price so that oil exporters would receive fair remuneration for their depleting oil reserves. He believed that nobody in the West was worrying about what would happen when oil ran out, and this was a drastic way of making them think about it. Dick told me of his concern that oil prices were going to rise dramatically. In December 1973 he sent a cable to Washington saying that the Shah was obviously thinking in terms of a new pricing arrangement that would peg oil prices to the cost of producing alternative sources of energy, such as oil from shale or solar energy. This idea, if approved by other OPEC ministers, would inevitably lead to an increase in oil prices. Current estimates of the costs of alternatives were $7 to $11 per barrel, which was less than the price sought by some OPEC members, who spoke of fifteen- to twenty-dollar oil.

The posted price (an artificial reference point) was raised to $11.65 a barrel at the December twenty-third OPEC meeting in Tehran. In terms of the average price paid by oil companies, this translated into a price per barrel of about $9.40. The revenues to Iran in 1974 were to increase to over $19 billion. This amounted to more than the total of Iran's oil revenues from 1908 through 1973.

The Shah talked constantly of his country becoming one of the world's five major industrial sites, excluding the super powers. He had a long way to go, and he worried about what would happen when Iran's diminishing oil reserves ran out. He talked about the need to build industry for exports, so that in the future Iran would have a way of paying for her imports. These were growing by leaps and bounds as Iranians became better off. They were buying more food, which meant more imports, because it was difficult to increase food production at home.

Iran's present and future wealth lay in its oil and gas fields and its almost totally untapped mineral wealth. The Shah believed hydrocarbons were too precious to be burned as fuel and Iran should go all out for nuclear-generated electricity. The first reactors were already being built, but they were costly; and because of the lack of water inland, seventeen out of twenty of the future reactors had been planned for the Gulf area. As this was an earthquake zone, it was a very controversial issue. There were also those who were afraid the Shah wanted his country to be familiar with nuclear capabilities for other reasons. After all, India and Israel were already able to build the atomic bomb, and Pakistan and Egypt were moving toward it.

Iran's arms buildup had begun in 1972, resulting in part from President Nixon's visit that year to Tehran. The British had withdrawn their forces from the Trucial States (now the United Arab Emirates) some months before, leaving a power vacuum in the Persian Gulf area which could be filled by a stronger Iran, the only friendly country in the area with the manpower resources to maintain a significant military establishment. In keeping with the Nixon doctrine (to help local forces rather than commit American personnel), the Shah would be permitted to buy equipment in the United States in amounts he felt necessary to become a decisive force in the region.

After 1973, Iran began enormous spending for military equipment and training. The Shah could defend this very eloquently when questioned. He was concerned about the sophisticated weapons given Iraq, which had about one-fourth of Iran's population, by the Soviet Union. Despite stories in the American press of huge Iranian military buildup, Iraq had more modern tanks and high performance aircraft than Iran. The Shah was also worried about the partitioning of Pakistan and made it clear that any military effort by India to further dismember Pakistan would cause Iran to take action on Pakistan's side.

In addition, the Shah was concerned with developments in Afghanistan where, in 1973, Mohammed Daoud unseated his cousin Zahir Shah and did away with the monarchy. Daoud was known as a convinced Afghan nationalist, but Iranians had the uneasy feeling that Soviet influence in Afghanistan was on the increase and that the Left might move at a moment of Russian choosing. In sum, the Shah increased his purchase of sophisticated arms from the United States, Europe, and the Soviet Union, and he was able to pay his bills from the great increase in oil prices.

The Shah had made a decision to supply his air force entirely from the United States. His policy was to purchase only airplanes that were in the U.S. Air Force or Navy inventory, thus assuring that there would always be available an adequate supply of spare parts. Efforts by the U.S. embassy and the U.S. Military Assistance Advisory Group to keep these purchases within bounds, and at a pace at which the Imperial Iranian Air Force could reasonably absorb them, were complicated by the tough competition among American aircraft manufacturers set on selling their wares. Heads of the big companies would see the Shah and attempt to talk him out of a recent decision in favor of a competitor or persuade him that he needed their particular aircraft in addition to what he had already agreed to purchase.

As for the Iranian Army and Navy, the competition was among British, German, French, Italian, and Russian arms makers as well as Americans. As I watched their cut-throat rivalry, I often wondered how the Iranians were ever going to put together a coherent force structure. This problem was not made easier by a Persian penchant for never wanting to admit ignorance, thus permitting in some cases an outrageous oversell by arms merchants. The American government role in this was minimal, we felt. Arms from the United States were bought through the Department of Defense's Foreign Military Sales. This in turn placed the U.S. government in the position of guaranteeing the arms' quality and performance. These arms were to be delivered over a long-term period, many taking up to ten years before delivery. The Shah, well aware of the bad publicity the rise in oil prices received in the world press, lectured his visitors not only on the finite limits of their oil reserves, but also on the large increases in the cost of American equipment. For instance, the cost of the American Spruance class destroyer that he had ordered for the Iranian Navy rose from $120 million in 1974 to $338 million by early 1976.

The Shah talked often of his concern for freedom of navigation in the Strait of Hormoz, between the Persian Gulf and the Gulf of Oman. These bodies of water constitute the southern borders of the country, and through the narrow strait pass Iran's entire oil exports as well as most of her key imports. Moreover, seventy-five percent of European and eighty-five percent of Japanese crude oil requirements transit the same strait. This narrow but vital channel was also the reason that the Shah gave military assistance to Sultan Qabus of Oman, a part of which protrudes directly across from Iran into the Strait of Hormoz. The Dhofar rebellion, whose insurgents used South Yemen as a sanctuary, were bent on the overthrow of the sheikhdoms in the Persian Gulf.

Iran's entire economic and industrial life depends on the ability of tankers to carry oil from her immense oil-exporting terminal, Kharg Island, to the rest of the world. The sale of oil is such a significant part of Iran's income that anything that stopped the flow would amount to economic strangulation of the country. The Shah wanted to be prepared should a hostile government of any kind come to power in the Persian Gulf. For many years he tried to create a mutual security pact with his neighbors, but the Arab countries were never willing to enter into written or oral bilateral understandings of this nature.

When we were invited to Kharg Island, Dick was anxious to go. The island was normally closed to visitors and only people invited by the National Iranian Oil Company could land there by plane.

We went first to Abadan, a city on the Persian Gulf. Abadan is surrounded by oil fields. Temperatures there can exceed 120 degrees in the summer and even during the winter it is extremely warm. Obviously a great deal of thought had been given to making the oil field workers as comfortable as possible. Abadan would have been a logical oil terminal except that it suffered from two serious defects: the shallow approach channel at the Shatt al-Arab and Iraq's nominal control of that same waterway. (The Shah had always at the back of his mind two things which his father had failed to accomplish. He often talked about them and his belief that they reflected on the sovereignty of the nation and his father's memory. The first was the nationalization of oil. This was accomplished during the Mossadegh period. The second was the border between Iraq and Iran in the Shatt al-Arab. The Shah commented to Dick one day, "That 1938 treaty which put the borders on our side of the river was demeaning, and I vowed to change it whenever I could. The chance finally came when I met Saddam Hussein in Algiers in 1975. He agreed to move it to the Thalweg in keeping with most riverine treaties between neighbors.")

Abadan is within easy range of mortar fire from Iraq, just as a gun placed in any of the many strategic locations near the Strait of Hormoz would stop the vast oil tankers from passing. The insurance on these ships is so great that no company would condone the unnecessary risk.

A sandstorm delayed us for two days. No planes would take off, and it was uncomfortable, if not impossible, to walk on the streets; you couldn't open your eyes wide enough to see where you were walking. We spent the time with the American consul, who had a comfortable house, an excellent cook, and a good sense of humor. The latter is particularly important during a sandstorm.

The small coral island of Kharg, thirty miles off the mainland in the Persian Gulf, is one of the greatest oil-exporting centers in the world. Six miles long and three miles wide, its backbone is a well-placed stony ridge running the length of the island. This ridge combines with the prevailing winds to form sheltered harbors. There is little arable land and the irrigation system of *qanats,* usually dug underground in the earth, had to be hewn out of rock. Arriving there you are immediately aware of two diverse elements of the island: the few evidences of ancient occupation—the remains of a Poseidon temple and Roman coins, a church with a Nestorian monastery, and the remains of a Zoroastrian fire temple—and the long lines of tankers waiting to fill up from the very latest in oil-port equipment. There are few local inhabitants not connected with the National Iranian Oil Company (NIOC). The ones you see are Arabs and often the women are wearing the conservative black mask across their eyes as well as the chador.

NIOC runs everything on the island. We were given a little cottage, one of the several guest houses. Our meals were delivered from a central kitchen and movies were available in the evening. A few government people took advantage of the facilities on the island for vacations as there is a good small beach, but of course there were no tourists. The Iranian workers were there without their families and they rotated continually. The expatriates, a breed who appeared almost stateless, were experts who moved from country to country and oil field to oil field and had their own camaraderie. They were used to the life: remote, hot, and a special type of living condition. They wouldn't have had it any other way.

In the morning Dick leaped out of bed to count all the tankers lined up. After breakfast we walked to one of the newest large storage tanks. An American met us and showed us around, telling us he had written his old engineering professor in the States about the mighty storage tank he had just finished. He gave the dimensions; the diameter was larger than a football field. The professor wrote back suggesting his pupil's measurements were wrong; it was impossible to build a tank that size, even in Texas!

The machinery on the island and on the deep-water loading area was clean and enormously complex. Small tankers were loaded on one side of the island and the large tankers were filled at an artificial island on the other. With all this tanker activity I could swim on the beach and rarely see a speck of oil. The government strictly enforced the requirement that oil tankers carry their water in compartments totally separated from the oil tanks so that when it was discharged it was not polluted with oil.

The terminal was extraordinarily vulnerable. There were miles of pipelines lying open on the desert, which could easily be sabotaged. Computerized control rooms loaded all the tankers. They were so efficient that a huge tanker could be filled in several hours. Apart from the visible security, underwater frogmen patrolled the bottoms of the ships to ensure against possible placement of a limpet mine to blow them up.

The trip out was through the narrow Strait of Hormoz, which was also the only sea passage for oil from Iraq, Kuwait, Saudi Arabia, Abu Dhabi, Qatar, and Bahrain.

Dick wanted to see the National Iranian Gas Company installations at Bid Boland and Ghachsaran. I wasn't enthusiastic; I didn't think visiting petrochemical plants or gas company installations would be very interesting. The flight proved me wrong.

It would have taken days to go by the only road available, so we went by helicopter, skimming over country so green and lovely it seemed almost unreal. We flew over hills and through mountain passes, wild and isolated country that made me think we were the only humans for hundreds of miles. But when at midday we put down for a picnic, we had hardly unpacked our food before we were surrounded by a dozen children. Where did they come from? I couldn't believe my eyes.

They were children of nomads, tribes that migrate across the country year in and year out, always moving and only settled for a season. Later I would learn more about the problem of the migrating tribes, but now as we ate our food I marveled at the beauty and the peace of these children and this place. As we took off I mulled over the contrast of the twentieth century intruding into this wild primitive land, and wondered which stood the best chance for survival.

The National Iranian Gas Company exported gas to Russia via a direct pipeline. Only a small percentage of Iran's gas is used even now, but it is a potential source of great wealth. Domestically it is used in the petrochemical industries or converted to fertilizer products that contribute to the nation's agricultural development. Most of this gas was the product of improved utilization of gas associated with oil production,

Migrating woman of a nomadic tribe.

and previously all of it had been "flared"—burned off at the wellhead. Much of it still is. The workers were well paid, comfortable, and the food was good, but the gas installations were so remote that the workers lived there without their families and were flown out every two weeks or so. We flew out too, again by helicopter, and I had time to reflect. We were visiting a refinery complex in the middle of nowhere, and we couldn't have seen this unspoiled, beautiful country in any other way except by helicopter. The juxtaposition produced startling, and continual, surprises.

From the air we spotted nomad tents, and came down for a closer look. These were of a Qashqa'i tribe, our pilot told us. They waved us down and, resting amid the camels and the black tents, our helicopter looked like a visitor from another planet.

School was in progress. The children were sitting cross-legged outside their white school tent, listening to their teachers. Older girls, black-haired and shy, were weaving carpets on the looms set up beside their tents. I sat on the ground beside the looms and watched them, but since they spoke a Turkish dialect we could only communicate by gesture. They were not pretty, but with their heavy dark brows and aquiline noses they looked aristocratic and strong. They dressed in layers of colorful skirts.

An old woman was spinning wool, sitting on the ground slightly apart from the others, and although it was impossible to tell her age from her weatherbeaten face, the speed of her fingers belied her wrinkles. Their housekeeping was minimal but immaculate. One of the older women invited me into the "dining" tent and offered me tea. What I wanted to see were the sleeping tents, but I knew I had to wait to be asked. I kept my back firmly to the men, who wanted to leave, and I refused to see their signs to me to hurry up. My patience was rewarded. I admired a flat-weave *gelim* carpet, and one of the women took me to see a finer one in her "sleeping" tent, its back and sides stacked with neatly folded bedding and more *gelims,* their own handwoven coverings for animals. The ground was covered with handwoven carpets. These nomads are not necessarily poor. Many of their chiefs are extremely wealthy and some may even own large tracts of land, often near their summer or winter quarters.

Before we left Tehran we had been asked to a Bakhtiyari wedding ceremony. This was considered a signal honor, and we decided to take the time to go. We flew for an hour by helicopter. Rifle shots greeted

us as we arrived in the area, scaring our security people into action, but
it turned out the tribespeople were only welcoming us. We were the first
ferangis, or foreigners, they had invited to that area. We went to pay our
respects to the head of the tribe, who invited us again to the wedding.
The ceremonies were to last for a week. The head of the tribe sent his
wife with us to call on his daughter, the bride, who looked exhausted
even though she was only halfway through the ceremonies. There were
hundreds of tribal people, the women dressed in their multicolored
skirts, all dancing and laughing and singing. We stayed for a picnic
lunch in a truly beautiful garden at Cheshme Belghais, sitting beside a
wide stream with the tribal leaders. A few spoke excellent English. As
we sat, they greeted guests, some of whom had traveled miles for the
festivities.

We were reluctant to leave, but we had a long journey to Bandar
Abbas, a bustling naval center and commercial port. I wondered if it
would be too far off to compare our reluctance to leave this remote area
for a modern city to Iran's tribes' reluctance to join the present. Was the
primitive past more inviting than the modernized present? Dick had
heard that Bandar Abbas was so jammed with ships and goods that the

A woman dressed in typical native clothing. I took this photograph while
attending a wedding near the village of Cheshme Belghais in southwestern Iran.

unloading was months behind schedule and the whole country was feeling the effects.

Only fifteen years before Bandar Abbas, controlled in the sixteenth century by the Portuguese, had been a small fishing village. Now we drove into the town on a four-lane highway. As we came close to the coast, we passed trucks lined up for miles waiting for cargo ships to unload. The new oil money had enabled the country to import enormous quantities of goods, but the various government ministries hadn't coordinated with each other. Available unloading docks and personnel were incapable of handling the traffic.

One of the ministers told us that each ministry had ordered enough imports to take over the port's capacity by itself alone. Ships queued up at Khorramshahr and Bandar Abbas sometimes as long as six months. By the time goods were unloaded, businessmen could not afford to pay the huge demurrage charges. The cargo ships had been held idle outside the ports for so long that the docks became piled high with unclaimed goods. Hundreds of trucks had been loaded when we were there, but there were not enough trained drivers to take them away.

The situation created a whole new industry. Businessmen arrived from the West with all sorts of schemes to bring cargoes off the stranded ships, at considerable cost of course, and the confusion at the ports engendered further problems: port authorities wanted to be paid off; work almost stopped during the hot summer months. The Ministry of Labor, in order to keep workers working, became involved in labor negotiations with them. The price of labor then soared as everybody involved wanted a share of the new wealth.

As we drove west we passed the large naval barracks, bustling with activity. Just outside the city we saw a line of trucks more than two miles long waiting outside a cement factory. Building had far outstripped the cement and steel supply.

Leaving Bandar Abbas to fly southeast you pass over the most desolate country, a geologist's delight, but there are no roads at all. Scarce water and grazing prevents habitation, even by nomads.

The Shah had decided to build a large naval base in the Gulf of Oman; he had aspirations to see the Iranian Navy become a military force in the Indian Ocean, and he had ordered four Spruance class destroyers from the United States.

The port of Chah Bahar with its beautiful natural harbor, the best on the Gulf of Oman, had almost become a legend. Getting information about it was like trying to catch a puff of wind in a mitten. Had it been started? Was it finished? There were conflicting reports. We went to find out.

We landed on a huge air base, still under construction. The Shah was building the air base for his air force and to service the future port. Concrete runways stretched out over the burning desert, more giant structures in a vast wasteland. The contractor, an Iranian friend of ours, had to import laborers from as far away as Azarbayjan in the northwest, South Korea, Pakistan, and other nearby countries. Every morsel of food and piece of equipment and housing had to be flown in, and different food had to be cooked to the tastes and religious laws of the different nationalities. Trucking in building materials was yet another challenge, as there was only one road in this area, from Zahedan in the north. It was so rough that every bag of cement was substantially lighter by the time it reached its destination.

We were driven a mile or so to a small town. The car was left in the parking lot for camels and we walked through the marketplace and down to the water. The Gulf of Oman was absolutely beautiful, calm, vast, and remote. There were none of the usual signs of a port. We swam at the beach and talked with an ancient fisherman sitting cross-legged mending his nets. He was agitated about the increased activity and didn't want the new port or the air field at all.

As the sun set that evening in a blaze of color across the sea, we could not help thinking what a mammoth undertaking building a naval base there was bound to be. (Even as recently as 1979 a young, well-educated Iranian talked about it to me and was astonished when I said to him, "There are no naval facilities at Chah Bahar.")

Flying north over the endless salt waste of the Dasht-e Lut you see little sign of life. To the east is Baluchistan and somewhere, a week's camel trek from the nearest dusty road, are the Baluchi tribal women, known for their beautiful embroidery. The Baluchis are impoverished Sunni tribespeople who roam the southeast area of Iran—a rugged, almost roadless land. An even larger number of Baluchis live across the roughly defined border in Pakistan, and to contend that a border really existed in that part of the world was to be needlessly legalistic. The Baluchis want an independent state, cut from both Iran and Pakistan. Both governments feared this independence movement because it was promoted and backed by the Soviets, who stood to benefit from any political change which would provide them with free passage directly south to the Gulf of Oman. Thus they would realize that centuries-old dream of Russian leaders, czars and commissars: a warm-water port for trade and commerce. Geographically it is also an area they would want to annex. So concerned was the Shah with this prospect that he sent helicopters to Pakistan to help Zulfighar Ali Bhutto put down unrest in the Baluchistan area. The threat to Iran and Pakistan from the Baluchi independence movement is no less real today.

On our way home the American consul took us to Yasuj to meet members of the small Boyer Ahmadi tribe. Fierce fighters throughout history, they had revolted in 1963, mostly at their leaders' instigation, because their land in a beautiful remote area in the foothills of the Zagros Mountains was taken during the land reform.

Now the government was hoping to settle the tribes by incentive rather than force. They had put up a sugar factory at Yasuj and started building roads, hoping the nomads would stop living by bartering and trading and become a part of the money economy. As we walked into the hills and drank *dugh,* a drink made from yoghurt, we played games, watched the chicken cooking on the grill, and listened to the tribespeople talk. Some of them seemed ready to accept a change; others were fiercely against any government program to change their way of life.

During the time I was in Iran I listened to many discussions about the migrating tribes—the problems of keeping their culture were complex. They needed their animal husbandry as a way of life, but it was sometimes argued the migrating animals did great damage to settled farmland as they crossed it twice a year. Could some members of the tribes participate in the migration each year, with a permanent settlement at both ends of the migration? Would this keep the tribes together and the people in good physical shape? Once more, there was a problem of ancient order caught up in and passed by the larger industrial forces. But viewing Iran today, this may not turn out to be the case.

14

Literacy and Rural Life

Man needs wisdom rather than gold.

Centuries ago Persia was known for its men of learning—Avicenna (Ibn Sina), Khayyam, Al-ghazzali—as well as for being a haven for philosophers and scientists from Greece and Rome. Why, then, did it ebb as a great center of learning?

The answer lies in the sweep of history. Power moved to the West, and new centers of learning arose in Europe. Persia's isolation grew, and she became for centuries a backwater in the so-called "civilized" world.

Persia was not only difficult to reach, but travel was hard inside the country. There were few roads, poor communication, and no real national education system. At the turn of this century there were fewer than ten thousand students in a hundred public elementary schools. There was only one high school in the whole of Iran.

Even after 1925, when Reza Shah pushed to develop the educational system, progress was slow. Of Iran's sixty thousand villages, only two thousand had schools. It was hard to find teachers for these remote areas, with their excessive heat, extreme cold, and no roads. In addition, the local mullahs had often taken over the leadership of the people, and they were usually against any sort of enlightenment.

By 1963 the solution of this problem was one of the six original points of the Shah's White Revolution. By the mid-1970s there were eight universities and more in the planning stage, and of the latter one was to be French-oriented and one German. All courses at Pahlavi University in Shiraz were conducted in English.

Unfortunately, the quantity of education improved more than the quality. The Shah recognized this and was surprisingly outspoken about the caliber of the university degrees, calling them "degrees of ignorance." Between 1974–75, when more than half the population of Iran was under seventeen years old, the total number of teachers in primary and secondary schools was about one hundred eighty thousand. Five percent of the teachers had completed primary school only, and about ten percent had graduated from college. This situation was also affected by the booming economy. The number of students studying abroad increased considerably, probably to as many as one hundred thousand by 1977. But not all the degrees earned abroad are superior to Iranian degrees. There have been instances in some countries where degrees earned by Persians have been awarded for less than the usual academic standards.

There were many problems in the universities and in the schools, including a limited use of textbooks, inadequate libraries, no commitment to research, and the disruptive student tensions and riots. But there were some areas of strength, particularly in medical education, engineering, and technology. I repeatedly met women who were chemical engineers.

The chancellor of Tehran University told me that half the students at his institution were from peasant families, but during my more than three years on the board of Damavand College I became aware that the students wanted a degree more than an education. This attitude was widespread. Students would go to any lengths to get their degrees. They would take the easiest courses and professors in order to do the least amount of work. Sometimes they would cajole the professors. If that didn't work, they offered bribes. The chancellor of a small college on the Caspian was almost beaten to death when he wouldn't allow students to take their final examinations if their attendance records didn't meet the requirements of the college. The students continued to take every possible holiday—three weeks at Now Ruz, one month for fasting at Ramazan, and many other unscheduled holidays.

There were few student clubs or organizations. Recreational activity outside the family, especially for girls, was limited; the men in the family allowed them such entertainments as *rowzeh khani,* where they listened to recitations of the lives of the martyrs, a traditional form of religious expressions considered safe.

There were institutions such as Arya Mehr Technical College where the Iranian professors are of high caliber and hold degrees from leading foreign universities, or the Iran Center for Management Studies, a Harvard-related graduate school, which offered an intensive eleven-month business course with eminent success. Damavand College developed from a two-year school to a four-year college, and the faculty hoped their graduates would fill leadership roles in their communities. Yet the Board found it difficult to find qualified Iranian teachers, and many foreign candidates were more interested in the high salaries of an oil-rich nation.

The Shah urgently endeavored to raise the quality of life of his people, not only in education, but in medical care as well. I sensed this particularly in the rural areas. For if the standard of living were to rise, public health and education outside the cities would be bound to improve—and an improvement in the standard of living for Iranian villagers was desperately needed.

Many doctors were working hard toward better medical care. Dick and I participated in a program for the new blood bank. The doctor who was trying to organize it told me that blood was needed badly, and we would lend credence to the program, which was new to the people. Many of the embassy staff joined us. Dick was the first to give blood and a large group of Iranians viewed the procedure to see if he survived. He did beautifully, but my driver, who wasn't at all sure about its merits, fainted.

So much of public health that we take for granted was unknown to the majority of Iranians. A Tehran pediatrician pointed out to me that if women were taught to sterilize their babies' bottles, ninety-eight percent of his clinics would be eliminated. He also urged women to wash fruit before they ate it or fed it to their children, because so many people became desperately ill from unwashed fruit in the summer months.

Hygienic practices had a long way to go. When I visited one hospital in Tehran, there were wards full of babies who had been circumcised with either dirty or blunt (or both) instruments. Their badly swollen genitals were a devastating sight. The chances of having a healthy normal baby in a rural area were limited, and to take that healthy baby and circumcise him in this way almost always resulted in fatal tetanus. There were many other babies with gashes on their hands or foreheads, supposedly to release evil spirits. The mortality rate of those babies was high.

The government planned vast health care programs for Tehran and other cities. A friend of mine from the Mayo Clinic came to Tehran and he told me some of the doctors at the Tehran hospitals were as good as he had seen anywhere in the world. But out in the villages the problems were different, since in many countries the doctors do not like to practice outside the cities. As you drive out into the country along roads or tracks where the landscape is dotted with Imamzadehs, the shrines of local saints or sons of Imams, you are very quickly in a primitive area. Years ago I had traveled and worked with medical teams that visited Jordan, Colombia, Algeria, and other countries and it was the same situation—even in the United States rural areas have trouble getting good medical care.

The Shah had created the Health Corps right at the beginning of his reforms in 1963 and 1964. Like the Peace Corps, many of the volunteers were dedicated young people who became well accepted in the countryside and were often of great assistance to the *kadkhuda,* or leader of the village. But they did not reach everywhere by any means. There were some new clinics and these were very successful, but the new hospitals had staffing problems, although the Shah and other VIPs were often misled by beds which would not otherwise be filled being occupied just for their visit. What was needed everywhere were skilled and professional people: doctors, nurses, and dentists. Indian, Pakistani, and Philippine doctors were imported, but they had to learn the language before they could be completely effective in either the clinics or the hospitals.

One woman I saw in a village told me her baby cried all the time. I was not surprised. So often we would see a baby being fed from a bottle that contained something that looked like weak tea. After a few questions, the woman showed me a tin of powdered milk she had been given from one of the new clinics in a neighboring village. It was a long way back to the clinic, and she could not read the directions on the tin; so she was giving the baby a very diluted formula. The poor child was starving. I convinced her that she must make it stronger, and when I came back a few days later she and the baby were all smiles.

A few of the young children had hip problems caused by sitting cross-legged on benches while making rugs. They do this at a very early age, sometimes as early as four years old, and often this causes problems with bone growth. A law was passed raising the age when a child could be employed in order to prevent young children from being exploited in this way, but of course it could only be enforced if the rugs were made in a public place.

At medical clinics in Tehran we were told that women were afraid of the IUD as a method of birth control because they thought it defiled their bodies. They were, however, happy to take the pill. In many Iranian villages the pill was dispensed without any controls, particularly if the clinics were busy or there was a dearth of trained help. Some Iranian women apparently believed that breast feeding a baby prevented pregnancy. An American I knew said she had studied many village women and this method did seem to work for them; most of their children were about three years apart. (A vet I know tells me this certainly works for cows!)

At times old and traditional ways seem to work very well for the

Children making a Persian rug in a village in the Caspian Sea area.

people. The childbirth process is relatively smooth. Still wearing her clothes, the village woman kneels to give birth to her baby, which is then caught from behind by the midwife. During labor the female members of the family crowd into the room and chant encouragement. The woman is usually very verbal and moves about, but she is encouraged not to lie down, as that is considered the most difficult position in which to give birth. There is a belief that boy babies, who are more welcome, appear faster than girls, who are said to be born face-up. The boys are born face down because they are not allowed to view their mother. Under all those clothes, who is to say if this is true or not?

After the birth, the bathing of the baby is an important ritual, because the baby is said to have been polluted by the mother's blood. After the placenta is expelled the cord is cut with a razor blade and left four fingers' width long. Nobody could explain the four fingers. Maybe it was started as a precautionary measure against the razor blade. Immediately after birth and the ritual bathing, the baby is cleaned and swaddled. Then the eyeblack, *kohl,* is applied. This has nothing to do with evil spirits (which are taken care of by amulets), but makes the eyes, so important in the East, more beautiful and powerful. After the birth the mother lies flat on her back for ten days, attended by her family. At the end of this time the midwife returns to take her to the *hamam,* the baths, for her ritual bath and to expel the evilness of pollution. No intercourse is allowed for forty days.

Diet in the villages was a matter I never understood. The people seemed to do well on their food and yet at first glance it seemed unhealthy. One scholar who had lived in a village for two years told me that although she had gone to study something quite different, she had become interested in the people's diet. They were very poor and she had begun by buying them meat as her contribution to the household; finally they had asked her not to because they didn't want it. They lived on rice, a lot of freshly baked whole wheat bread, a *khoresh* or stew with vegetables and a little lamb or goat's meat once or twice a week. *Panir,* or cheese made with goat's milk, and a lot of nuts are eaten all year round as they are dried for the off-season. My friend told me that she kept a store of tuna fish that she ate to supplement her own diet.

Ruth Stronach, the young Israeli wife of David Stronach, who wanted to film scenes of rural life and practices, asked me to accompany her. She wanted to watch a village woman building a new clay oven sunk into the ground and used for baking bread. We turned off the main road and bumped along a deeply rutted trail in our Land Rover until we came to a small village near Malayer. The small cluster of connecting mud brick compounds were actually separate entities, each housing an extended family that included the animals as well as the people.

As we made our way through the opening in the high wall past the goats and the donkeys, it was obvious that our arrival was quite an event. Most of the men had gone to work for the day and two handsome long-skirted young women were preparing to bake the bread over the coals in the old sunken clay oven. Each compound made its own bread.

The woman preparing to build the oven was delighted by all the attention and as she started the back-breaking job she told us she had had to go to a neighboring village to get the right clay. Only there did it have the right components. She described the other village with no name, but as a wealthy village: They had horses as well as donkeys.

After talking with a family we moved into the area where they kept the animals. Ruth asked why they had the animals in this area of the house, and the man, looking surprised, replied, "Because it is stronger and they are more important than people." The same shape as the other house, it was built with unfired pitched brick vaulting. Dr. Gus Van Beek, who was with us, was startled to note this and told us that this method of building goes back to the age of the Great Pyramids. In this modern village the brick work was based on the old Assyrian method used centuries ago.

With a promise that we would return again to the village, we bumped our way back to the main road. I did not expect to understand it all, but it seemed to me that in spite of the Shah's programs, the villages had not really changed much through the years. The education programs were beginning to work, and modern life had added radios and kerosene. But as one old man listening to his radio told me, "Tonight, according to the radio, we have everything." Then he added, "But tomorrow when I get up we'll have nothing again."

15

Progress Becomes Chaos

Pile up a load which can be drawn, not which can kill.

The Shah talked often and articulately about developing his country without distorting traditional values. He was convinced that modernization had to precede political development. But without a means of political expression the people had nowhere to go but the mosque, and both the sudden increase in development and the cash from oil brought surprising problems. Living in Tehran at that time, you felt surrounded by frenetic activity, spiraling higher and higher, like a twister crossing the desert. To become the accepted leader of the Middle East the Shah had one insurmountable problem: He headed a country that was almost entirely Shi'ite in a world of Arab countries predominantly Sunni.

Most of the people in the villages were illiterate, but they were not ignorant or unintelligent. With transistor radios, they were only a dial away from the news. (In later years television and movies, mostly Western, were widely available in the towns, showing Iranians a life they could not identify with.) They knew about the new dams being built to produce power. But many of them—even those as close as twenty-one miles from Tehran—realized that the dams brought them no electricity. The news did not tell them of the endless blackouts in the cities as more demands were put on the power system.

Under the Shah, industry grew in Iran and people from the rural areas left the farms, the harvesting, and the fruit picking to move into the towns, driving newly acquired automobiles over roads the Pahlavis had built (thirty-five years ago there had been only sixty miles of paved road in the whole of Iran). The roads soon became hazardous. Devastating accidents could be seen at frequent intervals, not on blind corners, but on straight desert roads. In Tehran some men found jobs as construction workers at wages far greater than those they had earned on the farms. But more ended up in a growing shanty town in the south of the city, living on the fringes of a culture they hardly recognized.

The construction continued apace until a cement and steel shortage brought it to a halt. The city had begun to look like a giant Mechano set, with huge cranes dotting the landscape. There were misgivings about the hurriedly constructed office buildings. An American architect I talked to had great doubts about their safety. He felt the buildings should be limited to ten stories because Tehran was in an earthquake zone. It was well known that many builders gave in to the economic temptation of sanding the concrete—there was certainly enough sand available—and it was definitely not the right mix for safety.

All the ministers and a handful of leading bureaucrats were vastly overworked. Most of the top people had trained abroad. They were very well educated and spoke a number of languages, but there seemed to be a minimum of trained people under them to carry out the mammoth plans. Even if you could get an appointment with a minister, foreign businessmen found their meetings frustrating. During the conferences they drank countless cups of tea and every phone call, however unimportant, was put through, causing endless distractions and poor use of time. Officials themselves admitted that in order to get anything done they had to follow through themselves.

The country needed technocrats and there was a drive to induce Iranian technicians to return from abroad, often at inflated salaries. Many who did return could not write, and sometimes not even speak their own language fluently. But it was an appealing opportunity. Many white-collar workers came back, joined by thousands of unskilled laborers from Third World countries.

Foreign businessmen flocked to Iran like bees around a honeypot, and Dick and I were kept busy racing to the airport to welcome heads of state from what seemed like every country in the world. It seemed apparent to me that some were there only to borrow money or to get a slice of the Iranian pie.

More and more visible were the German, the French, and the Japanese businessmen. It soon became evident that firms in European countries were strongly backed by their governments in attempting to get contracts, low-cost loans, and other assistance. We were constantly being asked to receptions to celebrate the signing of a contract with titled ex-royalty of European countries or British lords who had been sent in to add prestige to teams of negotiators.

Many small businesses, too, were successful in the early days of the new wealth. At a picnic I sat down next to a stranger, and in a glorious cockney accent he told me he had started a pencil factory. I asked him if he was making money. "I'm absolutely coinin' it," he replied. "I don't even have to get up in the mornings any more."

American companies did well because there was great regard for American technology. The U.S. military assistance group grew as the Shah bought more and more arms. The number of Americans in the country increased to well over forty thousand. Competent and highly respected in their fields of expertise, few knew much about Iran. There had been little in American newspapers about the country in the last decade. James Bill, a scholar of Iranian history from the University of Texas, pointed out that in the *New York Times* during the period of 1965–75 there were 195 references to Iran as opposed to 1114 discussions of the internal affairs of Israel, and 263 references to Ethiopia.

So many problems developed in the American community that the embassy started a program of orientation for the families. It was strongly suggested to the U.S. companies involved in Iran that they brief and prepare families that were being sent over. The companies soon saw the need for this when it became very costly to return families unable to make the Iranian adjustment. As usual, the wives bore the brunt of the changes. They often came ill prepared for the Eastern culture and, if they were stationed outside Tehran, the lack of schools and recreational facilities for their children. For the military the change was not so intense. One general told me he had visited the air bases in the country and was proud to claim that he had never left their confines!

In Esfahan the fifteen thousand Americans had little help, and their isolation was difficult for them. In Tehran it was easier. The families had

the ever-expanding Tehran-American School and the American
Women's Club. I came to admire and respect these women who gave
companionship and support at troubled times. For recreation, there were
classes in everything from the Persian language to belly dancing. They
printed a telephone book in English and ran trips to every country you
could think of—and some you never thought you would think of. They
conducted tours in the city and around the country to orient new arrivals.

With the boom came inflation. Houses, if you could find them, were
renting for up to four thousand dollars a month for three or four bedrooms. Hotels practiced a bird-in-the-hand reservation system and
often did not honor prepaid reservations. To combat this, companies
started to keep rooms permanently. I received many frantic calls for help
from acquaintances. One woman from the World Bank came to stay at
the embassy after declining to spend a third night in the Hilton Hotel's
broom closet.

Housing was a terrible problem for the average Iranian as well. Property values were impossible and rents were so inflated there was little
low-cost housing available. I followed the agonizing lack of progress of
one family trying to find something larger than the one room they
occupied. In 1976 a bus driver told me that he had been offered more
than thirty thousand dollars for his house—two small rooms, an outside
toilet, and no inside running water. The two tiny rooms were heated by
a kerosene lamp. They cooked in an outhouse beside the toilet; there
was one burner for the whole family. But they did have electricity.

The economic problems affected everybody. The rich, of course, grew
richer. But even though the minimum wage was increased twice to a
considerable figure, inflation dogged the rising expectations of the poor.
They were able to buy more, but the quality of goods dropped as the
prices rose. With a new social security act, everybody received more
money, but the money could not buy what people wanted most. For one
thing, their own local produce was no longer available at any price. The
panir-e tabrizi was replaced by cheese from Bulgaria, and *dom siyah,* rice
from the Caspian area, so much better and preferable to the imported
rice, was almost impossible to find. Frozen imported meat was a new
idea and no one liked it. One of the reasons people couldn't buy the
local produce was that government money was committed to imports
rather than domestically produced food. Also, there were too few people on the farms to pick the fruit and harvest the wheat.

Going to the large vegetable and fruit market at the southern end of the city became a ritual. Dick's driver, Heikaz, always took me, but I liked to shop by myself and do my own bargaining and buying. During one period onions had become scarce in town, a disaster because you cannot cook Iranian food without onions. We had been without them for weeks and my chef had challenged me to find some. After much searching, I found a sack of them tucked away at the back of a stall. I opened the sack to take a look and while I was asking the price several women wearing chadors attacked. I felt they were about to peel me and the onions. At last I was able to explain in my halting Persian that, given the opportunity, I was quite prepared to share the onions with them.

During the summer of 1975 Dick and I realized that there was a financial crisis. Businessmen were complaining that they were getting only partial payment on contracts, and I was receiving telephone calls from Americans who said they were not being paid at all. By the end of the year the situation was worse, with many projects delayed. Students returning from the West to work rarely had their aspirations fulfilled. This was obviously a personal and unexpected humiliation for the Shah. There had been a wild spending spree and a great deal of money had been wasted. For the first time the growing corruption of the country was discussed openly.

Members of the royal family and many others became involved in business deals as projects were started which cost vast sums of money. The overworried ministers grew more servile as the Shah became more authoritarian and less available to his people. The coterie of fixers around the ministeries, armed forces, and the royal family flourished, and corruption grew to huge proportions, despite sporadic attempts to control it by the Shah, Prime Minister Hoveyda, and others. They failed because it seemed impossible to change time-honored Iranian "business methods." The contracts were so large that even a very small payoff was considerable.

There has been much speculation as to whether the Shah was aware of the problems, although they were increasingly evident to those of us free to travel around the country. The senior officer in the Iranian Navy, personally picked by the Shah to help build the service, was sent to prison for kickbacks and corruption. The Shah learned the facts of some of the payoffs when hearings in the U.S. Congress were held regarding American involvement. Dick told me that the Shah seemed visibly shaken by the unexpected magnitude of the problems and no longer lectured his visitors on the decadence of the West with the same conviction.

Under the Shah Iran, for the first time in its history, had a central government whose laws had an impact. They were obeyed more or less by all except in the most remote parts of the country. Since 1962 the Shah had increasingly taken the tradition of Persian kingship and its responsibility as *farmandeh,* or commander, more seriously. The Shah-People Revolution that he had begun alone, and single-handedly developed, included not only land reform, but also price controls, free education, and other ideas that he believed would better the lot of the Iranian people. The government had to carry the burden. Who else would have started schools in the remote areas? Many Iranians were definitely better off, and for those who cared the Shah had given back to them their national self-respect. They were becoming a nation no longer under the thumb of foreign domination.

However, because of the monarch's role throughout Iran's history, the government had never had to achieve a consensus from the people: The art of popular persuasion was new to the leadership. The few who attempted to develop a separate following soon found themselves out of office and into oblivion.

The opposition to the Shah and his programs came mainly from three sources. The religious leaders disliked him for moving toward a secular state, for giving women the vote, for trying to diminish their own wealth, and for developing an educational system that reduced their own influence, particularly in the villages.

The second opposing source was the student population. Now that there were more schools in the countryside, increasing numbers of young people were coming into the towns; but they soon found they could not get into the universities. There was just not enough room, and teachers could make more money as construction workers. One young man told me that the living money the Shah provided for the students was in fact "vodka money," so they would drink and forget their criticism. He said that the students who went to America were forced to stay there so that nobody clever would be left in Iran. I was besieged with requests to help obtain visas to the United States. The embassy was processing thousands every month, particularly for students. I continually explained that I had no authority where visas were concerned and that I could not place favorite sons at the head of the constant queue at the consulate. Visas were entirely a matter for the consular officers.

In order to facilitate the long lines of applicants that started forming as early as three in the morning, the consular offices were expanded to near the main gate of the compound. But within a few days we discovered that the Iranian policemen assigned to keep order were selling places in the line.

The third opposition group included those affected by government interference. Bazaar merchants, traditionally very powerful, felt unhappy because they had lost out to banks as the center of financial trade. The wealthy businessmen were often exploited. For example, they might be obliged to purchase expensive villas on the resort island of Kish. The less affluent also were unhappy. The Shah's insistence on importing technology, industry, and foreign advisors made middle-class Iranians feel inferior.

The Shah had created such a one-man show that many people wondered what would happen if he died or became incapacitated. Perhaps realizing that it was no longer possible for him to hold all the reins himself and also because there was a lot of pressure on him, the Empress began to play a larger role, taking part in discussions and even encouraging forums for criticism of government programs. Criticism of the educational system was one of the things that was openly discussed, and her warmth and desire to listen and learn gained the Empress much respect.

One minister told me that members of the royal family would listen to him only if a project was in their interest. The Empress, however, tried to read and study in order to understand what was being asked of her. But she still seemed unable to shake the Eastern tradition, and she appointed relatives and close friends as directors of welfare projects and Iranian bureaus; three new museums were headed by her cousins. All favors were bestowed from the top, so it was helpful to be close to a member of the family or one of their close friends. Even ministers found it easier to get financing for projects that way. Foreign and Iranian businessmen were quick to realize that a contract was much more likely to be considered if one of the inner circle backed it. Many people explained to me that all their troubles would be over if I would just consent to bring their particular problems to the attention of the Empress.

But even the Empress's endorsement of a program was not enough. Her fine art collecting was a classic example of the confused way things could go wrong. When the Empress had determined that a fine arts museum should be created, she supported it with intelligence and enthusiasm. Her advisers, however, were not all so well motivated. The museum's acquisition budget was considerable, but many foreign dealers saw petrodollars coming their way and manipulated their prices to absurd levels, even for the inferior pictures the museum purchased. An art expert told me that when the staff tried to catalogue all the paintings, it was impossible to determine how much had actually been paid for any one picture, and because of this it was hard to get insurance for the collection. There was also no reliable list of what pictures had been acquired, although many of the canvases were by such painters as Renoir, Toulouse-Lautrec, and Picasso. To make matters worse, nobody seemed to know where many of the pictures were stored. Eventually some turned up in a warehouse near the Tehran bazaar in unbelievably filthy condition. No heat or humidity controls existed in the warehouses, and many pictures had screw eyes put in directly against the painted surfaces. Two massive bronzes by Henry Moore were found in vast packing crates said to contain road-working equipment.

The Shah, almost as if to oil the wheels of his total power, sometimes announced policy decisions in the most quixotic way. One day while I was out food shopping I ran into all sorts of people rushing in and out of shops. The Shah had just decreed free milk for all school children, with no prior notice. On another occasion he suddenly decreed the change of the year, from 1355, the date according to the Hegira calendar of the Moslem religion, to 2535, dating from the coronation of Cyrus the Great.

In March 1975 the Shah took people by surprise when he announced the new Rastakhiz party. It would have conservative and progressive wings which would provide him with information. It sounded like a possible way to collect the country's available energy into one channel. I asked one party official, a very busy man, how he would have time to organize anything that would bring the people's thoughts and desires to the attention of the party, and eventually to the Shah. I was skeptical because people were too scared of Savak to say what they thought, even to their families.

Foreign firms, in their search for contracts, brought with them much that Iran needed, especially technical knowhow and management skills. But they found only a small number of Iranian businessmen who were competent and reliable. Thus a few Iranian families became enormously wealthy. Inevitably these families extended and diversified their interests and empires and attained a reliable reputation among American businessmen.

The shortage of skilled labor spurred some Iranians to improve their own facilities, and Dick and I visited many factories with training programs and support facilities that Westerners would have envied. One of the most striking features of Iran in the mid-seventies was the number of items fabricated locally—textiles, cars and trucks, household appliances, steel and aluminum. In 1947 Iran had only 175 large industrial plants, but by 1972 there were over six thousand. The growth was not always efficient, but compared to many surrounding countries the Iranians learned quickly and made a lot of progress. There were, after all, hard-working people in the country who were not involved in corruption and who loved their country passionately.

The Shah began to realize that some of the pitfalls he had hoped to avoid were now upon him. But he continued to believe he could bring a better life to all Iranians. Perhaps he took heed of what had been written over a thousand years ago: "The King is like the Sun and it is not worthy of the Sun to shine on some and to withhold light from others." He announced that private businesses would have to sell forty-nine percent of their shares to employees or permit public participation. This had an unexpected effect, and not only on wealthy businessmen. It sent their foreign joint-venture partners into a tailspin. What did the Shah's decree mean? Business fell off heavily while everybody tried to decide. It was at this time that wealthy Iranians started to transfer huge sums of their personal wealth abroad.

Shortly after this, shopkeepers were harassed by youths who, under official auspices, tried to stop overpricing and other ills. Many shopkeepers and businessmen were arrested for profiteering and some left the country. Some were exiled internally, a form of punishment used since ancient times. As a result, these same bazaaris later supported the Ayatollah Khomeini with enthusiasm.

We lived constantly in the shadow of the most active of the anti-Shah dissidents, the urban guerrilla movement. Seven people were attacked and killed while we were there—six Americans and one Iranian, the latter mistaken for the American he had set up for assassination. The last three killed, employees of Rockwell International, were shot on August 28, 1976. In a car on the way to work they were ambushed and murdered, shot with forty-two bullets at point-blank range.

16

Protocol of a White House Visit

From whichever quarter the wind blows he will winnow his grain.

In some respects 1975 was a difficult year for me. It brought the hearings of the Rockefeller Commission and the Senate Select Committee on Intelligence, chaired by Senator Frank Church, which delved into the twenty-five-year-old history of the CIA. Dick, as a former director of Central Intelligence, was asked to testify a number of times, and it seemed to me that every time I looked around Dick was either taking off for Washington or returning. Scheduled plane arrivals in Tehran were always very late, which made delayed flights even later, and I spent many hours waiting for news of Dick's planes. The flight from Washington was never less than seventeen and a half hours in those days, and he sometimes made the round trip in four days. To testify after such a long flight was grueling, and I knew it put him under great pressure, particularly when there is an eight-and-a-half-hour time difference between Tehran and the United States.

It was difficult for me to fathom exactly what was going on. I was naturally apprehensive about some of the stories that were being spread across the newspapers of the world—charges that the CIA had behaved like a "rogue elephant" and that the agency was responsible for the assassinations of foreign leaders. There appeared to be endless allegations of misdeeds and abuses of one sort or another. We talked for long hours while Dick explained to me the origin of some of these allegations. That these charges were not nearly as serious as they sounded at the time emerged later, but Dick was very concerned about the damage the various exposures were doing to the U.S. Intelligence effort. The only time he got very upset—furious, really—was when the allegations of assassinations were reported as actual assassinations.

When he was head of the CIA, he was tangentially, if not actually, aware of most of the events under investigation. He remarked on one occasion with a wry grin that he sometimes wondered whether there had ever been anybody else in the agency who had been responsible for anything. He had pointed out to me many times during our marriage that when you take on a controversial issue there are always a lot of supporters, but they are only prepared to hold your coat.

It was particularly difficult to be six thousand miles away from him while he was testifying. Even though he telephoned every day, the connection was sometimes terrible, and we both knew that an international telephone circuit, particularly from an embassy, could not be counted on to be secure. Those were the days when we were more than usually grateful for the support of all our friends. Living under the strain of the guerrillas and the hearings, I sometimes had nightmares. I awoke one night when Dick was in Washington to what I thought was the sound of a shot. Convinced that I was about to be kidnapped, I leapt out of bed, grabbed my nightie, and rushed to the door. When I got back into bed I realized I had grabbed only my second-best nightie. I was anxious not to embarrass members of the embassy staff if they did have to rescue me. I was about to get out again and change it when I realized my foolishness and started roaring with laughter. I tried to keep my sense of perspective, but I wondered later what the marine on guard duty thought when he heard one lone ambassador's wife roaring with laughter in the middle of the night. Maybe he knew there were many lonely days and long nights at that time.

In the spring President Ford invited the Shah and Empress to Washington. An ambassador always accompanies a head of state, and so both of us were to go too; it was a great relief for me not to be left behind. The preparations began weeks in advance. The plans were, of course, up to the President and the Shah to announce.

Unfortunately, the Shah's old school in Switzerland, Le Rosey, was planning to hold its alumni reunion in Iran on the exact dates of the visit to Washington. They had enlisted the help of the government of Iran and members of the court and were very much hoping the Shah would receive them. One of the organizers came to see us, since Dick had also attended Le Rosey. The school suggested we might entertain them at the time of the reunion. But the school's officials had to be turned down without explanation; we could not tell anyone until the Shah officially announced his plans that we would all be out of the country. Aside from this disappointment, everything went smoothly.

We departed for Washington a few days before their Majesties were expected to arrive. They went to Colonial Williamsburg, Virginia, to rest after first visiting Mexico and Venezuela. In Washington, Dick and I decided to stay at the Hay Adams Hotel near the White House, because we had learned during the last state visit that it was impossible to find time between events to go home to change.

Accompanied by the U.S. Chief of Protocol and his wife, the Shah and the Shahbanu flew from Williamsburg by helicopter to the White House. To the tune of ruffles and flourishes and the two countries' national anthems, they were welcomed on the south lawn by President and Mrs. Ford, an invited group of guests, and a horde of news photographers looking for endless "photo opportunities."

Following this traditional ceremony, we all left almost immediately for Secretary of State and Mrs. Kissinger's luncheon at Mrs. Merriweather Post's spectacular estate, Hillwood. The luncheon was served under a large tent, placed so the guests had a panoramic view of Washington.

Like most official guests, their Majesties stayed at Blair House opposite the White House on Pennsylvania Avenue. State visits are a grueling experience for the participants; in between all official functions they each receive delegations and participate in media interviews. The Shah met with the President alone. Although he had a large official group with him, including his Foreign Minister, he preferred to conduct official business himself, and when he went to his meetings in Congress only Dick and Ardeshir Zahedi, the Iranian ambassador to the United States, accompanied him.

The state dinner was held at the White House. We arrived fifteen minutes ahead of the guests and went upstairs to the Yellow Oval Room, the sitting room in the private quarters of the President and his family. President and Mrs. Ford went downstairs to meet their Majesties and brought them up to the Oval Room for cocktails. The rooms had all been redecorated since we were last there, and it was interesting to see how each President's wife changed them. Dick had been in the family quarters often, and once he had taken me around on a tour. President Nixon had not entertained in the family quarters, and I had not been to a party upstairs since President and Mrs. Johnson had invited us to a small farewell party.

After an informal and friendly few minutes, during which the Shah decorated President and Mrs. Ford, Dick and I withdrew. Protocol required us to go downstairs to the East Room and the official reception. The foot of the grand staircase descends into the foyer, where we were met by marines ready to escort the ladies to the East Room. There the other guests for the dinner had gathered, dressed in white tie and evening gowns. It was an elegant and distinguished dinner party.

A few minutes later the marine band began the dramatic and traditional ruffles and flourishes. The President and the Empress, chatting amiably, descended the wide curving staircase, followed by the Shah and Mrs. Ford. At the door of the East Room they were announced, dramatically, to the now quiet crowd of waiting guests. They entered the room to a rousing rendition of "Hail to the Chief." It was a spine-tingling moment.

The Shahbanu wore a white, three-tiered sparsely beaded chiffon dress, created by the Italian designer Valentino. Her hair was pulled back softly into a chignon, which was not only very becoming to her but showed off her large turquoise and diamond earrings. In 1973 she had been criticized in the press for wearing too much jewelry; this time she was amused when, the following morning, she showed me a newspaper report reproving her for wearing too few jewels.

Mrs. Ford, in a pale yellow long-sleeved dress, was warm and charming as the four principals received. They greeted old friends and exchanged a few words with each guest. We walked past members of the press; they were not invited to attend the dinner but were assembled behind a roped-off area in the foyer. Marines, looming splendid in their full-dress uniforms, lined the hall. Big tubs of flowering pink and white dogwood trees decorated our way into the state dining room, where we took our seats at beautifully set up round tables.

When the Shah visited Washington, his wife danced with Fred Astaire at the
White House. Dick and I are dancing at left.

We were served salmon gélée with sauce verte, saddle of veal with tomatoes Saint Germain, Spinach en branch, salad and cheese, and praline mousse. The wine was good by anybody's standards—a Riesling 1970 served with the fish and a 1971 Cabernet Sauvignon with the veal. The Air Force String Players walked among the tables playing romantic melodies while dessert was served.

The President rose to give a lengthy toast, to which the Shah responded. These toasts were piped into the press room for the waiting journalists. The dinner was followed by a few brief moments of conversation in the Blue Room. Then the after-dinner guests joined the party, which was continued in the East Room. The entertainment was a bit astonishing—a Las Vegas-type show at which Ann-Margaret danced in red, white, and blue tights, followed by four male tumblers. This concluded, there was a brief farewell with glasses of champagne, and Mr. and Mrs. Ford escorted their Iranian guests to the front portico for the short drive to Blair House.

The next day Dick went with the Shah to Andrews Air Force Base for a demonstration of airborne warning systems and to the Pentagon for a meeting with the Secretary of Defense. I and other members of the official group accompanied the Shahbanu to a luncheon given by my old boss, Dillon Ripley, at the Smithsonian Institution.

At home and abroad the Shah and his wife were constantly besieged by requests for money. Almost every caller or host seemed to shake hands with his right hand while holding a proposal for funds in his left. Hence, the invitations were numerous.

Following our visit to the Smithsonian, we went to Georgetown University, where the Empress was to receive an honorary degree. (The Pahlavi Foundation gave money to a number of universities in the United States for the support of Persian language departments; as this money is no longer available, many of these departments have either ceased to exist or are much reduced in size.) During the speeches we could hear anti-Shah demonstrators outside. The speeches at Georgetown and throughout the American visit were delivered with strange pronunciations of *Shahbanu;* the dignitaries found innumerable ways to articulate the word, some of which defy description. One official, in cap and gown, outdid all the others with what sounded like *Shahbanger.* (The correct pronunciation is Sha-ba-nóo). I wished they had been coached in advance or advised to use the word *Empress,* but it was a minor problem compared to the griev-

ances of the demonstrators outside, some of whom turned out not to
be Iranians.

The Shah and Shahbanu gave an all-Persian dinner for President and
Mrs. Ford at the Iranian embassy, and a special group brought from Iran
for the occasion presented folk dances and played traditional Iranian
music. Eastern music is not easy for Westerners. But this performance
was by the very best players, who used a *santur* (an instrument played
with hammers), an *ud* (a lute), and a *dombak* (a drum). The performance
was excellent and just long enough.

When the official meetings were over, we flew to Tarreytown, New
York, where Vice President and Mrs. Nelson Rockefeller gave a small
dinner at their estate, Pocantico Hills. Rockefeller drove the Empress
around the vast riverside grounds in a golf cart to look at the hundred
or more pieces of sculpture situated in acres of manicured gardens.
There wasn't a drooping plant in sight, but I teased the Vice President
by pointing to a dead branch at the top of one tree. It was the only sign
of a vegetation blooper in the whole place.

Rockefeller also showed us a small Japanese house on the estate that
he had built and hoped Mrs. Rockefeller would live in after his death,

During their Washington visit, the Shah and Shabanu were the hosts at a dinner
in honor of President and Mrs. Ford at the Iranian embassy.

because the big house would become a museum. It was a friendly, relaxed time, after the hectic pace of the last few days. Traveling en masse in an official party that is of interest to the press is hazardous. You are apt to get trodden on, or knocked flying by large camera equipment in the hands of people much more interested in their "photo opportunity" than in the lives of intervening human beings. The lady in waiting to the Empress was rather tiny and delicate, and frequently I found myself running interference to save her from being knocked down.

The Shah and his Empress left for home that night from New York, and we returned to Washington for a few days to visit our children before we, too, boarded an overseas plane. On the long flight back to Tehran, what stood out most clearly in my memory was the talk. What a joy it was, in comparison to Iran, to hear everyone freely expressing their views, even opposing ones. Just to talk and listen to relaxed, thoughtful, critical, and creative discussions was music to my ears. Like many another American living abroad, I wanted to shout back through the skies to tell my countrymen, "Look what you have! Look at what you can say out loud and no policeman will stop you!" A fatuous desire, perhaps, but that is the way I felt.

17

Full Circle

Water which runs downstream does not run upstream.

In the late spring of 1976, shortly before we began preparing for the Fourth of July celebration, Dick told me he had been thinking about our return home. He said he had received a message from Henry Kissinger informing him that the Secretary of State would be coming to Tehran in August. Dick went on to say he thought we should decide what we wanted to do by then as it would be a good time for him to discuss it privately with Henry rather than having to send a cable, which, even if he used the secure channel, would be read by a number of people. He suggested that I think about it for a few days and then we would take the time to sit down and discuss it quietly. Dick said if he was going to resign he was anxious to do it officially before the November election, so that it could not be misconstrued and look as if he did not wish to serve the next President, whoever he might be.

Sitting in our beautiful garden, looking at my own special mountain, with Farooq waiting on us, I reluctantly agreed with Dick that by the

New Year in 1977 it would be time to leave. We had both had enough of official diplomatic life. I knew that whenever we left I would do so with a sense of things unseen and friendships just beginning, and only a brief brush with a Moslem culture.

In the meantime, we plunged ahead with our plans for Independence Day. There would be a big picnic that representatives of American businesses in Iran coordinated for the whole community, as well as our own reception at the residence. This year Luigi and I had planned an all-American menu. He had agreed to make hundreds of small rolls in which we would serve little hamburgers. Celebrations like Christmas (when we organized carol-singing parties) and the Fourth of July are very important when you live abroad.

On July 1 we received a phone call from the Israeli representative in Iran. He said he was sorry to be rude and hoped we would understand; he would be unable to attend our reception. A normally calm, extremely intelligent man, whose company we always looked forward to, he sounded unusually agitated. We wondered what was disturbing him.

The Shah, heading a Moslem country, could not have official diplomatic relations with Israel, but the Israeli trade mission in Tehran operated very much like an ordinary embassy. After all, Iran's two hundred thousand Jews were not recent immigrants; they had settled in Iran during the Second Babylonian Empire and had encountered little prejudice down through the centuries. The Shah encouraged this course; he had been heard to say that neither Israel nor Iran wanted to be surrounded and alone in a sea of Arabs.

A day or two later we heard the news of the Entebbe raid when Israel flew troops into Uganda to rescue their citizens being held hostage. We wondered if our friend had been involved. Sure enough, he returned to Tehran immediately and we were able to hear an exciting first-hand account of the operation.

Henry Kissinger arrived a few weeks later. To have him as a house guest was quite an experience. He had come twice before while we were in Iran, and on these official visits virtually the whole embassy, as well as protocol officers of the Iranian Foreign Office and the Foreign Minister, turned out at the airport to greet him and his considerable entourage.

The work and planning involved in these visits was nothing short of horrendous and I watched with awe what went on. A horde traveled with the Secretary of State on the official airplanes, and I realized that

In 1974 Secretary of State Kissinger and Nancy Kissinger paid an official visit to Iran. Here they chat informally with the Shah and Shahbanu and Dick and me.

all those people had to be housed and fed, their clothes laundered, and their dollars exchanged for local currency for the shopping that they wanted to do.

The biggest requirement was the installation of extra communications, not only for the bevy of tired reporters, but also for the official party. Instant secure communication with the White House was essential. By 1976 the security problem was intense. Many times on official visits from Washington bullet-proof cars were sent ahead by plane. Occasionally the security was burdensome. Cables flew back and forth between Tehran and Washington about who was to be included at various functions. The number of places at dinner tables became international issues with senior officials, some of them senior enough to make it unseemly that they insisted upon being included.

Everywhere I went in the embassy residence there were Secret Service men. Henry's sense of humor and the warm friendly atmosphere he and Nancy both created saved the day. On this particular visit Nancy had just had surgery for a stomach ulcer and was drinking nothing but ginger ale. We had had cables to this effect, but I had been all over town and this was the week there was no ginger ale to be found. I was delighted when she came down the plane stairs carrying a six-pack of the elusive elixir.

The residence staff had to be calmed as the endless flow of aides and secretaries wanted sandwiches or something other than the food we served. Probably through past experience they had decided sandwiches were safe in a foreign country. But to a chef who prided himself on his clean kitchen and the fact that we had never had a sick guest, this was a little upsetting.

Kissinger, taking advantage of the geographic location of Iran, summoned American envoys from surrounding countries to confer with him in Tehran. He had meetings set up in many different rooms, and he would move from one to the other. At one point he announced that he wanted to buy a carpet, although Nancy said she was not sure she wanted one. I had a man bring some to the residence, but he didn't care about selling the carpets. All he wanted was to have his photograph taken with Henry.

Kissinger would eat anything put in front of him, and as Iranians feel hospitable only if they feed you every few minutes, he consumed a lot. He made the stewardess of the Shah's plane very nervous, as any complaint probably did.

"Where have you been?" he said to her during one flight. "I haven't eaten for ten minutes!"

As Henry admitted, he worked best under pressure, and if something had to be written he usually started at the eleventh hour. His sense of humor was spontaneous and superb, and almost always unfailing. I say "almost" because I watched him in his large official airplane, calling in aides, who sat poised with yellow pad and pencil. One after the other they arrived to listen to the boss, and there were times when his sense of humor was dropped for another approach. Under those circumstances I noticed that Nancy quietly picked up her book and read attentively as if nothing were going on around her.

Kissinger seemed completely tireless and often we retired for the night before he started work in his temporary office in the embassy residence. Obviously his staff was ready for this. He seemed to have a constant coterie of pale, exhausted-looking young men around him, who would take him on in shifts.

The first thing he wanted when he came down for breakfast were the newspapers. "If I'm not on the front page," he said to me one morning with a laugh, "my father will be worried."

The only time I saw Henry unhinged was when we went to the Caspian Sea and he was taken to a caviar factory. There in one-hundred-degree heat a technician proceeded to cut open a sturgeon to take out the caviar. Henry blanched. He hadn't wanted to go there anyway, but his distaste was obvious. His face assumed a pale shade of green and I thought he was going to be ill.

Because of the increase in traffic problems that made traveling in Tehran a time-consuming event, as well as the concern over security, the Shah gave Henry the protection of the Imperial Guard, a distinction usually reserved for visiting kings or chiefs of state. He also put at the Secretary's disposal two helicopters with his own pilots. It took flying prowess to get them in and out of the embassy's small grassy area which was surrounded by telephone and electrical wires. But the pilots were skillful. One copter would land and discharge its passengers. Then it would quickly back up out of the way and the other would land. This went on endlessly morning, noon and night, as people went back and forth to meetings and social functions.

After the visit to the caviar factory, we went to a guest house at Nowshahr. There we were received by the Shah and his Empress for luncheon. As usual, delicious fresh fruit juice was served, in this case watermelon and pomegranate juice. There were large bowls of fresh, peeled walnuts on ice and those habit-forming seventy percent fat and carbohydrate pistachio nuts that the Chinese in the eighth century had referred to as "the hazelnut of Persia." Served fresh and peeled, they are irresistible.

As I sat beside the Shah and listened to him talk about international politics, I realized how almost European he had become. He had brought his country into the modern world, but in doing this he seemed to have removed himself from its heritage. He came to think of himself as a world leader, and he enjoyed nothing more than discussing international affairs with other leaders of stature. But as he moved into this role, Islam became a religion to him rather than the way of life it is supposed to be. Even as a religion, he was no longer outwardly committed to its principles. For many years he had written and talked of a Supreme Being who protected him and gave him divine guidance to carry out his "mission" for his country. He believed he had a direct relationship with God. Deeply religious in his own way, he felt God was communicating with him. But he was psychologically independent of any religion and certainly didn't need any intermediary. He did not go to the mosque or share a time of prayer with his people.

In this he was not alone. After I had lived in Iran for a while, I realized there was something about the mosque that many of the government leaders feared. At that time, three years before the revolution, I did not sense a fear of an uprising, but rather of physical danger. In recent years, assassinations had taken place inside the mosque, including two prime ministers. With the crowds and the chador to conceal any weapon, it was an ideal place for violence. But apart from physical danger I don't believe the Shah thought he needed to be seen worshiping in public. He seemed sure he had fulfilled his religious duty by renovating the shrine. Photographed beside a shrine, he would always be standing alone, perhaps in prayer, but symbolically and physically separated from the mass of pilgrims.

After luncheon the Shah, Kissinger, and Dick adjourned for a discussion. I had often heard Henry talk about his admiration for the Shah's understanding of world problems. Dick, too, enjoyed his many conversations with the Shah for the same reasons, although doubtless there were many times in which they did not agree.

Nancy and I went to the Shah's residence on an inlet on the Caspian a short distance away. The official designation of any residence the Shah

Dick and I buy fresh pistachio nuts in a village near Yazd. Eaten shortly after picked from the tree, pistachios are indescribably delicious—and habit forming!

The Empress, Nancy Kissinger and I have a meeting of our own while our husbands confer during the Secretary of State's visit to Iran in 1974.

occupied was a palace, but this small villa built on stilts over the water was hardly that. The royal family kept boats there for waterskiing, and their children were able to have friends there for vacations. The Empress stressed the importance of these holidays together, not only as a pleasure but as training for the children. The Crown Prince was expected to have an awesome role ahead of him, and there was considerable concern for his training. At that time he spoke no English at all. Since then he has studied in the United States, recently as a student at Williams College.

Nancy and I joined a group of bikini-clad friends that the Empress had as guests, including former King Constantine of Greece and his wife. The Empress invariably had a group of her own particular friends around her. They were usually the same people. Some she had known at school and almost all were friends of long standing whom she was obviously comfortable with. The Shah similarly had his card-playing friends. But he seemed impatient with his wife's friends and regarded them as a coterie of chic sycophants.

Henry's favorite place in Iran was Esfahan. He was fascinated by the mathematical and decorative intricacies of the mosques. He thoroughly confused the travel guide assigned to him because he didn't swallow the guide's usual line of tourist patter and wanted things explained with considerable care.

A mosque, or a place where one prostrates himself, comes from the Arabic word *masjid.* It is the place where one fulfills one's obligation to perform prayers, laid down in the Koran for all Moslems. On Fridays at noon the prayers are said as a collective act by the community. During Mohammad's time, when he was the leader of these prayers, it was also a time of communicating activities with believers. Though still controversial, scholars think the mosque design derives from Mohammad's private house in Medina. It had a large courtyard with two shaded areas, and in the early days of Islam this space, used for the public gathering of the Moslem community, was transformed into a building.

The *mihrab,* or niche, is always described as the mosque's focal point, designating the direction in which one turns to pray; but it is now thought that the *mihrab* honors the place where the prophet stood when leading prayers, commemorating his presence as the first Imam.

The *quiblah,* or wall, indicates the direction of prayers. In front of this wall there is always a pulpit where the religious leader pronounces the *khutbah,* which is not only a sermon but an act denoting the community's allegiance to its leader. Mosques have no chairs or anything else (except sometimes Persian rugs) to divert the community from their prayers.

There are no high mountains near Esfahan. As you come to it across the bleak and barren land, the town rises up as the heart of an oasis formed by the Zaindeh Rud, the only great river of the plateau. Of all the cities in Iran, Esfahan gives the appearance of flourishing. It was considered one of the world's most perfect cities, but it was on the verge of losing its beauty to steel mills, new bazaars, and modern city planners when we visited it.

Toward the end of Kissinger's visit, Dick told the Secretary of State that he wanted to resign and to return home. He planned to send in his resignation in the fall and he asked that it be announced before the approaching presidential election. Kissinger agreed, but the announcement wasn't released until the night before the election.

Dick and I felt greatly enriched by the opportunity we had been given to live in Iran. But not until the moment of departure did we admit to each other that, however long we stayed, we would never fully understand the country or the people. As our plane took off for Washington,

The Lutfellah Mosque, built by Shah Abbas, overlooking the Royal Quadrangle in Esfahan in central Iran. It is one of the most perfectly proportioned domes in Islam. (LYNN SALMI)

I looked back over our four years in Iran and wondered how I could ever have not wanted to come; it had been an extraordinary experience.

My first day in Washington I went early in the morning to the store to buy food for the house and ran into an acquaintance. She pushed a petition in front of me, saying "Sign this. It's to save the seals." I asked if I might take it home and read it before signing it; I hadn't thought about seals for four years. Crossly, she declined and said if I wouldn't sign it right away it was no good. At that moment Iran seemed light years away; I felt as if I had come down from Mars. Now I needed time to catch up with America.

18

Postscript: Fallen Monarch

It's what you have that counts, not what you used to have.

On January 16, 1979, while thousands of people massed in the center of Tehran to denounce a fallen monarch, Mohammad Reza Pahlavi Shahanshah Aryamehr left his country, never to return. The following month, the Ayatollah Ruhollah Khomeini returned to Iran after fourteen years of exile to claim that the nation, by the popular will of the people, would now become an Islamic republic.

Thus ended the Pahlavi dynasty, a royal rule that had looked back to the golden age of Persia to remind Iranians of their heritage, but had lasted only fifty-four years, a mere moment in the long history of Persian existence. The vision of the Shah and his father for a new Iran had been inspired by Western progress and economic development. But the Ayatollah would have none of it. He claimed civil and religious authority to lead a revolution that would return Iran to fundamental Islamic Shi'a doctrine.

Why did the Shah fall from power?

If you ask an Iranian, you may be told that the United States was responsible for the revolution; or perhaps the British will be accused; or the Russians; or the Israelis. Indeed, Iranians believe that the Shah was overthrown because of intervention from abroad. That is the story behind Iranian history. No historic event occurs without a conspiracy involving foreigners. In addition, in modern times they considered that the Shah and his father had brought about the Westernization of their country without the guidance of Iranian Islamic theologians, as stipulated in the 1906 Constitution. All the reasons an American might adduce to prove that the United States did nothing to help the revolutionaries would be unavailing; those brown Iranian eyes would glaze over.

If you ask Americans what happened to bring about the Shah's downfall, the reasons given vary, and there is no essential agreement about the relative importance of the many elements. Certainly all the facts are not yet in, and may not be for many years. So let me touch on those factors which contributed to the dissatisfaction of the Iranian people.

In the Shah's push to modernize Iran, he did little to provide vehicles for political expression. Amir Taheri, a political journalist, wrote in the newspaper *Kayhan* late in 1978:

Had the bazaaris had political parties of their own, they could have used the nation's accepted and legal channels of decision making to air their grievances and pressure the government into meeting their demands. But no such vehicle was at their disposal. As a result they did what they had done on numerous occasions in the past: used religious organizations and leaders for political purposes.

Under the Shah, most Iranians feared to speak their minds, afraid that Savak would report them. There was nothing new about this in Iranian modern history except that an increasing number of the Western-educated young hammered away at the issue of repression in a society becoming increasingly affluent and increasingly subject to foreign influence and propaganda. Into this atmosphere came the religious harangues against the Shah from the Ayatollah Khomeini and his followers in exile in the form of audio cassettes smuggled into Iran. The agreements reached between Iraq and Iran in 1975 eventually opened the border between the two countries, permitting ten thousand Iranian pilgrims per year to cross over to the Shi'a shrines in Iraq. This gave Khomeini, then

4rt October, 1973.

Dear Mr. Ambassador,

I thank you for your letter of 3rd October 1973 which I have had the honour of submitting to the High Attention of His Imperial Majesty The Shahanshah Aryamehr.

My August Sovereign is deeply touched by the sincere sentiments which you and Mrs. Helms have conveyed following the discovery by the Grace of God of the heinous and dastardly plot against Their Imperial Majesties, The Shahanshah Aryamehr and The Empress and His Imperial Highness The Crown Prince.

I have been commanded to express to you and Mrs. Helms His Imperial Majesty's High Appreciation of your friendly gesture together with warm wishes for your welfare and happiness.

With high esteem and kindest regards,

Yours sincerely,

Assadollah Alam
Minister of the Imperial Court.

His Excellency
The Honourable Richard Helms,
Ambassador of the United States of America,
Tehran.

In September 1973 a plot to assassinate the Shah failed. Dick wrote the Shah to express the relief of the U.S. government that His Majesty had not been harmed. The Shah's Minister of the Imperial Court responded with this letter.

in exile in Iraq, contact with the pilgrims. What had been a trickle of Khomeini propaganda into Iran became a flood.

When the anti-Shah disorders started in Tabriz in January 1978, the mosques and the bazaars began a collaboration which filled the streets of Iranian cities with countless demonstrations for months to come. Certainly the Shi'ite clergy showed a singleness of purpose that emerged with clarity in 1980. Indeed, there are those who contend that Khomeini had a *doctrine* of revolution, and that the philosopher of the revolution was Ali Shariati, a former professor at Tehran University who died in London in exile during 1977. Be that as it may, Shi'ite fundamentalism threw the whole weight of its opposition against the Shah, thus providing religious sanction to the efforts of secular, leftist, and intellectual forces who were fighting him as well.

I think Dick put it accurately in a short article that he wrote in 1979:

When rioting and demonstrations began in Iran early in 1978 and continued until the Shah's departure in 1979, many disparate and competing elements rallied together under the rubric "Down with the Shah." His thirty-seven years of rule had focused so much attention on his person that blame for most of the faults of Iranian society were put on his account. It became clear that significant elements in the country, many of them not religiously motivated, banded together spontaneously to force him out.

It is interesting to note that when the chips were down, the Shah had no constituency. Perhaps the Imperial Guard or the army could have acted as substitutes, but for reasons which have not yet clearly emerged, they collapsed in the end, or conversely, the Shah never really called on them. The Shah forgot the age-old Persian homily that a king who does not command cannot be considered a king.

I returned to Iran twice; Dick went back three times. He happened to be there at the time of President Carter's visit at New Year 1978. We were there together for the last time in June 1978. The Iranian friends we visited at that time were very perturbed about the general evidence of unrest, but they were not yet ready to predict what was likely to happen.

In the last year of his reign, it became clear that the Shah's cancer had progressed significantly. Perhaps psychologically he equated his illness with that of his close friend and associate for many years, Assadollah Alam, one of his few advisers who could be counted upon to tell him the truth. Alam had died of leukemia in the spring of 1978. The Shah was, according to people who saw him frequently, taking a lot of medicine.

Dick saw him and talked with him alone. The Shah said he could not understand the conflicting signals he was getting from Washington.

We had lunch alone with Amir Abbas Hoveyda, who had been appointed Court Minister, and later with the Prime Minister, Jamshid Amouzegar, who was concerned about the large sum of money that one of the ministers had ordered transferred to the United States that very day, despite the Shah's request that money not be sent out of the country. But the Prime Minister was relieved that the Shah had finally agreed to limit the participation of the royal family in business deals. He hoped that this would halt the criticism as well as the corruption, which had grown to outlandish proportions. But it was far too late.

What happened during the next few months is difficult, if not impossible, to unravel. Washington was intensely occupied with the Camp David negotiations that President Carter was conducting with Menachim Begin and Anwar Sadat. Although we were receiving many calls from Iranians on their crisis, there was no publicly perceived Iranian emergency.

After months of turmoil, opposition leader Shahpur Bakhtiar was finally given approval by the Parliament on January 16, 1979, to form a cabinet. As had been agreed upon earlier by the Shah and Bakhtiar, the Shah left the country, ostensibly for a long vacation. As he boarded his plane, the Shah said, "I hope the government will be able to make amends for the past and also succeed in laying foundations for the future." After a brief stay in Egypt, Morocco, the Bahamas, and Mexico, he was given permission by the Carter administration to fly to New York City for medical treatment.

On February 14, 1979, the U.S. embassy in Tehran was attacked by revolutionary groups. Guns were fired from the apartment house behind the tennis courts into the ambassador's residence. By this time it was becoming public knowledge that these guerrilla groups had been trained by the Palestinians in Syria, Lebanon, and Iraq. This accounted for the accuracy of their marksmanship and the disciplined nature of their operations.

The servants took refuge in the ambassador's apartment, only to give up as the revolutionaries approached up the stairs. The consulate was besieged and eventually occupied. Negotiations with the Iranian government resulted in representatives of the two main revolutionary factions remaining for some months in the embassy compound.

Again, on October 27, various revolutionary groups occupied the U.S. embassy for a few hours. Finally on November 4 they returned to occupy the entire compound, holding sixty-six Americans hostage and causing three other members of the embassy staff to be detained in the Foreign Ministry. Thirteen of these hostages, the blacks and many of the women, were released and allowed to go home. Members of the staff who were not in the main chancery building at the time of the takeover managed to escape from the consular building where they were working. They went into hiding and six of them were eventually repatriated in January 1980, with the help of the Canadian embassy in Tehran.

Late in the Shah's confinement at a New York hospital in 1979 Dick and I went to call on him. His bitterness over the behavior of his former Western allies kept intruding on our conversation.

"Why did you want to destroy what we had?" he asked. This was in reference to his conviction that the Carter administration wanted him out of the way and a new government more to its liking to replace it in Tehran.

"Why was General Huyser [Deputy Commander of U.S. forces in Europe], a U.S. Army officer, sent to Tehran by your government? What were his instructions? Why was I not informed that he was coming? Why was he meeting with the generals of the Iranian Army? Why did President Carter's wife write to the Empress, assuring us of American support, if you did not mean it?"

But an even greater sadness seemed to envelop him over the behavior of General Hossein Fardoust, who as a boy had accompanied him to school at Le Rosey and as a man had enjoyed his total confidence. "He was more than a brother to me," the Shah said emotionally. It was clear that he regarded General Fardoust's accommodation with the Khomeini forces as treason.

I asked why the Shah had chosen to leave his country. He seemed surprised and replied, "To avoid bloodshed. That is the difference between a king and a dictator."

He continually returned to the theme of "why did you do it?"

"The real difficulty was caused by too precipitate liberalization," he said. "The Americans and the British kept pushing me; they wanted a democratic republic. They wanted me to be more liberal with my opponents. The changes were genuine on my part. But Iran is not ready for Western-style democracy."

As we left he said, "Alam died at the right time."

We did not see him again. He died in Egypt on July 27, 1980, having been granted political asylum by the humane and courageous act of President Anwar Sadat.

In November 1979 a plebiscite in Iran approved a new Constitution that announced that a monarchal system is contrary to Islam. Since then, the changes made by the Ayatollah Khomeini have affected all political, social, cultural, and economic policies in Iran. Under the new Constitution the Ayatollah has named himself the Velayat-e Faghih, who until the reappearance of the twelth Imam (who allegedly "disappeared" in the ninth century) will pronounce on what is allowed, *halal,* or forbidden, *haram,* under Islamic law. This is Khomeini-style Shi'ism.

Part of the Constitution says that the Islamic Republic of Iran shall be presided over and represented by a leader and Imam, who will be a religious purist as well as an honest, virtuous, knowledgeable, courageous, and efficient administrator, enjoying the confidence of the majority of the people. This has been interpreted to mean that even Parliament can be overruled by the Faghih, or Philosopher King.

In Islam, democracy has usually been of a consultative nature between the leaders and the people. Now it is in the Constitution that the Faghih knows best the teachings of Islam.

The mullahs have taken over the judicial system and the civil law is being revised in light of Islamic teachings. The universities have been closed in order to review the scholastic programs and to bring them in line with Islamic teachings. All mixed schools have been sexually segregated and all bilingual schools have been closed. Only the religious colleges are flourishing.

The purging of citizens with any Western connection has included the sophisticated technicians running the oil fields, although paradoxically some of the returning revolutionaries have strong Western ties. Many managerial- and professional-class citizens have left the country. Workers have been encouraged to take over the management of factories. In the absence of skilled management, spare parts and raw materials were in short supply. However, because of this there has been a return of agricultural workers to the countryside. Although oil production has fallen considerably, the current high cost per barrel produces a national income from oil that is still high.

Now that the Shah is dead and the country is once again in the hands of the mullahs, we may wonder what will be the future of this ancient land. To me, Iran—this glorious Persia—can be likened to its native cypress tree, a symbol of wholistic life. In a storm, it may submit to the wind, but it survives, returning to its original position when the wind has ceased. In this storm, I believe Iran will survive as a country, as it has for thousands of years.

> Think in this batter'd Caravanserai
> Whose doorways are alternate Night and Day
> How Sultan after Sultan with his Pomp
> Abode his Hour or two, and went his way.
> —OMAR KAHYYAM

Index

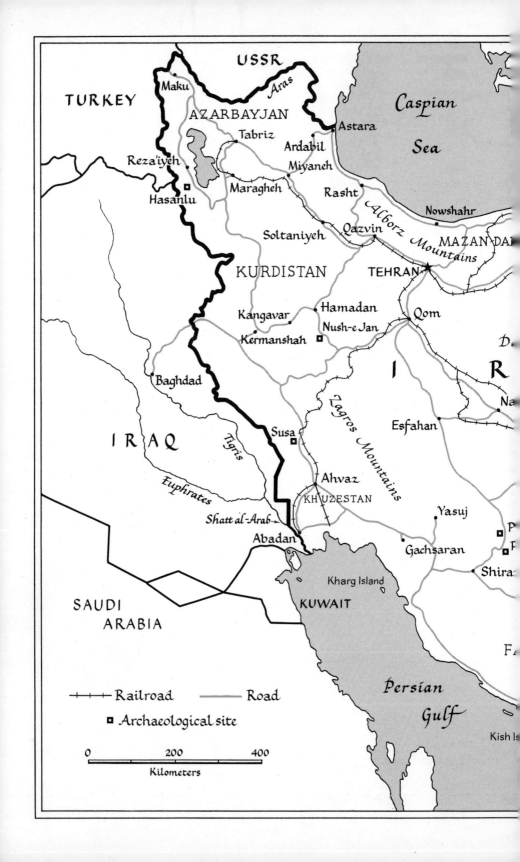